W9-BPC-552

HBR Guide to
Coaching
Employees

Harvard Business Review Guides

Arm yourself with the advice you need to succeed on the job, from the most trusted brand in business. Packed with how-to essentials from leading experts, the HBR Guides provide smart answers to your most pressing work challenges.

The titles include:

HBR Guide to Better Business Writing

HBR Guide to Coaching Employees

HBR Guide to Finance Basics for Managers

HBR Guide to Getting the Mentoring You Need

HBR Guide to Getting the Right Job

HBR Guide to Getting the Right Work Done

HBR Guide to Giving Effective Feedback

HBR Guide to Leading Teams

HBR Guide to Making Every Meeting Matter

HBR Guide to Managing Stress at Work

HBR Guide to Managing Up and Across

HBR Guide to Negotiating

HBR Guide to Networking

HBR Guide to Office Politics

HBR Guide to Persuasive Presentations

HBR Guide to Project Management

HBR Guide to
Coaching
Employees

HARVARD BUSINESS REVIEW PRESS

Boston, Massachusetts

Copyright 2015 Harvard Business School Publishing Corporation
All rights reserved
Printed in the United States of America
10 9 8 7 6

The web addresses referenced in this book were live and correct at the
time of the book's publication but may be subject to change.

Library-of-Congress cataloging information forthcoming
ISBN: 978-1-62527-533-2
eISBN: 978-1-62527-538-7

The paper used in this publication meets the requirements of the
American National Standard for Permanence of Paper for Publications
and Documents in Libraries and Archives Z39.48-1992.

MIX
Paper from
responsible sources
FSC® C132124

What You'll Learn

When you're swamped with work, it's hard to make time to coach your employees—and do it *well*. But if you don't help them build their skills, they'll keep coming to you for answers instead of finding their own solutions. That kind of hand-holding kills productivity and creativity, and you can't sustain it. In the long run, it eats up a lot more time and energy than investing in people's development.

So you really must coach to be an effective manager. Got a star on your team who's eager to advance? An underperformer who's dragging the group down? A steady contributor who feels bored and neglected? With all of them, you'll need to agree on goals for growth, motivate them to achieve those goals, support their efforts, and measure their progress. This guide gives you the tools to do that.

You'll get better at:

- Asking the right questions before you dispense advice

- Creating realistic but inspiring plans for growth

- Providing the support employees need to achieve peak performance

- Tapping their learning styles to make greater progress

- Giving them feedback they'll actually apply

- Giving them room to grapple with problems and discover solutions

- Engaging your employees and fostering independence

- Matching people's skills with your organization's needs

- Customizing your approach

Contents

Section 2: COACHING YOUR EMPLOYEES

Section 3: CUSTOMIZE YOUR COACHING

Introduction: Why Coach?

by Ed Batista

After graduating from business school, I was hired by a founding board of directors to launch a new organization, the Nonprofit Technology Enterprise Network. I had shared a leadership position before, but this was my first time as a solo chief executive, and I believed it was my responsibility to come up with the best ideas myself and champion them aggressively.

This approach led to a number of conflicts with my directors. A mentor of mine on the board took me aside and said, "We think you're a talented young guy, but you have some rough edges. We'd like you to invest in yourself and get a coach." One of my former professors had a coaching practice, and I asked her to take me on as a client. That was one of the best things I've ever done.

Although few coaching clients ultimately decide to become coaches, as I did, my positive experience of coaching is typical. The tremendous growth in the field over the past 20 years has been driven by consistent reports from clients who feel more effective and fulfilled as a result of the coaching they've received. And it doesn't help only at the individual level. Although researchers can't yet precisely measure coaching's effect on organizational performance, numerous studies (published in the *Journal of Management*, *Consulting Psychology Journal*, and other publications) show a positive impact.

Being coached helped me understand that I could make the biggest difference as a leader not by doing more than everyone else but by empowering other people to do more and motivating them to do their best. This meant letting go of certain responsibilities and recognizing the limits of my expertise. I didn't need to have all the answers; I just needed to ask the right questions. In short, I came to realize that effective leadership looks a lot like coaching.

But what do we mean by *coaching* in the first place? The simplest definition is "asking questions that help people discover the answers that are right for them." A more specific definition that applies to you as a leader and manager is "a style of management primarily characterized by asking employees questions in order to help them fulfill their immediate responsibilities more effectively and advance their development as professionals over time." The emphasis on *asking questions* is noteworthy when we consider that conventional leadership roles typically position the leader as the expert, someone who *provides answers* and whose domain knowledge is one of the foundations of her authority. In contrast, when a leader acts as a coach, she needs to adopt a different mind-set and add value in different ways.

It's no coincidence that the increased demand for coaching has accompanied the shift from command-and-control hierarchies to flatter, more distributed organizations. In the 1950s, management thinker Peter Drucker coined the term *knowledge worker* to describe a newly emerging cohort among the white-collar ranks; today most professionals fall into this category. Because they require (and desire) little or no direct supervision and often know more about their tasks than their managers do, knowledge workers usually respond well to coaching. Unlike directive, top-down management, coaching allows them to make the most of their expertise while compelling them to stretch and grow. As their manager, you set overall direction for them—but you let them figure out how best to get there.

Many senior managers and HR executives have come to view coaching as an investment in high potentials or as a perk for stars. Others still see coaching mainly as a corrective measure for underperformers. Daniel Goleman noted in his classic *Harvard Business Review* (HBR) article "Leadership That Gets Results" (March–April 2000) that despite coaching's merits, it was used least often among the management styles he studied. Leaders told Goleman that they didn't have time to coach their employees, and you may feel the same way. But coaching is broadly applicable, and managers at all levels can benefit from working with their direct reports in this way. You may need to encourage those around you to participate—and you may need to be persuaded yourself.

If so, I urge you to give it a try and gauge the return on your investment. Although external coaches like me will always play an important role in supporting leaders and their teams, coaching shouldn't be our exclusive domain. It's an essential management tool, and there are circumstances when a "coaching manager" can be more useful than a professional coach. I often help clients reflect on difficult experiences in order to make sense of what happened and extract some learning, but these conversations occur days or even weeks after the event. A leader who has coaching skills can help team members begin to reflect on a difficult experience immediately. Highly skilled leaders can even facilitate these discussions with their entire team present, allowing everyone to learn simultaneously. When leaders view coaching as the sole purview of external professionals like me, they miss countless opportunities to add value.

My experience as a coaching client, as someone who teaches coaching to MBA students, and as a professional coach has shown me the value of coaching as a management technique, and a large and growing body of research reinforces this conclusion. It takes time and effort, but the material in this guide will help you integrate coaching methods and processes into your own management style.

There's no "right" way to coach, so you'll have to decide for yourself which approaches described in the chapters that follow work best for you and your direct reports. Like any new skill, coaching requires practice, and you'll need to step outside your comfort zone as you experiment. Don't be too quick to write off a technique just because it feels awkward at first.

Coaching presents every manager with challenges. You may have to reconsider your leadership style and the ways in which you add value. You may feel reluctant to surrender control or to give people room to make mistakes, and you'll almost certainly be tempted to jump in with solutions when they're struggling with a problem. But those challenges get easier the more you coach, and the payoff is enormous: You'll tap your employees' full potential while leading more strategically.

Last year a client who'd founded a successful company concluded that his management style was holding back the firm. He and his senior managers had so many tactical responsibilities that they weren't truly leading. They were putting out fires, with a limited capacity to take a longer view and make the systemic changes the business needed.

So my client decided to restructure his role, delegating some tasks to his senior managers. He coached them as they assumed these duties, prompting them with questions to solve problems in creative new ways rather than simply telling them what had worked in the past. They, in turn, took the same approach with their direct reports.

As a result, the company's management team raised its sights and focused on more-strategic issues, which had a positive impact on the business. And my client found that he was actually more productive while spending less time in the office. When he sold the company and stepped down from his leadership role, he left with confidence that the management team would adjust seamlessly, and the business has continued to thrive.

That's what's possible when you coach your employees. That's why it's absolutely worth your time. And that's why you'll find this guide an invaluable addition to your leadership reading.

Ed Batista is an executive coach and an instructor at the Stanford Graduate School of Business. He writes regularly on issues related to coaching and professional development at www.edbatista.com, and he is currently writing a book on self-coaching for Harvard Business Review Press.

Section 1
Preparing to Coach Your Employees

Chapter 1
Shift Your Thinking to Coach Effectively

by Candice Frankovelgia

Do you ever say to yourself (or others), "This person just doesn't get it" or "This person will never have what it takes"? If so, you may have what Stanford psychologist Carol Dweck calls a *fixed mind-set*, which will severely limit your ability to make a difference as a coach. Low expectations rarely yield growth and often lead to frustration on both sides. You may occasionally encounter someone who truly can't develop, but the real barrier is most often *the belief that the person won't make progress.*

Adapted from the Center for Creative Leadership's course "Coaching for Greater Effectiveness." For further information, visit www.ccl.org.

It's easy to fall into this trap. After you've acquired a lot of experience and knowledge in your field, doing things yourself may seem simpler and faster than helping your direct reports improve their critical thinking, technical, or organizational skills. But that's a short-term solution that leads to long-term problems. If you keep providing all the answers, people will keep lining up at your door looking for them.

Shifting Your Mind-Set

In the end, it's actually less time-consuming to embrace a *growth mind-set*—one that assumes your people can learn. If you invest in their coaching and development early on, you'll reap benefits later: They'll start solving more of their own day-to-day problems, freeing you to focus on strategic issues and developing more leaders.

Shifting to a growth mind-set takes effort. In the coaching workshops I teach to managers, participants talk about how hard it can be at first—but once they make the switch, they start seeing better outcomes.

An R&D director at a manufacturing company had an employee who struggled to give clear, concise, organized presentations. When that person asked for input on a draft slide deck, the manager's impulse was to mark it up with suggestions to reorganize the information and cut down on the length. But then she caught herself. She called the employee in for a conversation and asked clarifying questions: What are the key points you want to convey? How much does your audience already know? What points will be difficult for people to grasp? If you were in their place, would this presentation help you reach your goals? What can you do to bring it more in line with what your stakeholders are hoping to achieve? With renewed energy and focus, the employee went back to work and improved the presentation without heavy-handed intervention from the manager.

A growth mind-set can feel risky because it forces you, the coach, to develop skills of your own that go beyond subject-matter expertise. You must ask questions and really listen without jumping in to provide what you believe is the "right" answer. And you must be honest about the performance you expect and where your employee stands, to make sure you're on the same page about the development work that needs to be done. Otherwise, you're resigning yourself to the status quo—so why even bother to coach?

Sharpening Your Coaching Skills

Here are the key skills you'll need to hone before you can help others learn and grow:

Reconciling intent and impact

You can gauge an employee's impact on the organization by observing him in action and using performance metrics such as satisfaction surveys and sales figures. But you won't know his intent—the driving force behind his behavior—unless he shares it with you.

When employees underperform, there's often a gap between intent and impact, and that can lead to great misunderstanding and frustration. Coaching them effectively involves clarifying their intent so that you can close that gap. How? By asking them what impact they *meant* to have. For instance, you might say to someone, "You were quiet at the last sales meeting—can we talk about why?" You and others may have viewed his silence as resistance or disengagement, but perhaps he was just trying to cede the floor for a change, knowing that he can be domineering in group discussions.

Once you've asked the question, listen closely to the answer. (See the sidebar "Active Listening Tactics.") Discuss behaviors that confuse or surprise you, especially those that don't match the intent he describes.

ACTIVE LISTENING TACTICS

Pay attention. Build rapport by giving your full attention. Maintain comfortable eye contact and an open posture (avoid hunching, crossing your legs, or hunkering behind a desk). Be genuinely curious. Allow time and opportunity for the other person to think and speak. Avoid distractions such as e-mail.

Notice nonverbal cues. "Hear" the speaker's nonverbal messages and body language. Do the tone of voice and facial expression match what's being said? If not, comment on what you notice and ask your employee to tell you more about it.

Affirm what you hear. Indicate understanding: "I hear what you are saying" or "I'm following you. Could you say more?" This simply means that you are listening closely—not that you agree.

You're likely to miss out on critical information if you find yourself:

- Talking more than listening

- Suggesting solutions before the employee has the chance to do so

- Interrupting

- Thinking about what you want to say next instead of focusing on what your employee is saying

Reflect what you see and hear. Reflect (like a mirror) the other person's emotions without agreeing or disagreeing: "You seem worried about . . ." This encourages the speaker to express feelings and deepen exploration.

Paraphrase what you hear. Periodically restate basic ideas to check your grasp of key points: "If I understand, your idea is . . . Did I get the essence of it? If not, please tell me more."

Summarize key themes. Briefly sum up the other person's point of view to show you've listened and to check your understanding: "It sounds like your main concern is . . ." or "These seem to be your main points . . . Is that right?"

- Using body language that signals impatience or distraction—checking your e-mail, accepting phone calls, leaning back in your chair

- Saying what you would have done differently in the same situation

As a rule of thumb, ask more than you tell—aim for a ratio of about 4:1. If you flip that ratio, you're teaching, not coaching. Though teaching plays an important role in developing others, it's limited to what you know. Coaching is an interactive opportunity to discover and create previously unknown solutions. (See the sidebar "Teaching Versus Coaching.")

Always assume positive intent, even when dealing with difficult behavior. People usually mean well—and if you give them the benefit of the doubt, they'll be more forthcoming about their intent and more receptive to feedback.

Recognizing your biases

Your own preferences can get in the way of discovering others' intent. Maybe you have a gut reaction against certain personality types or struggle to identify with colleagues whose work styles differ from yours. Whatever your biases, recognizing them allows you to move past them by inquiring about intent rather than jumping to conclusions or filling in the blanks.

To spot your biases, use frustration as your guide. Think about what gets on your nerves at work and then ask a few trusted colleagues for feedback. What do they think your bugbears are? Compare their thoughts with yours—look for similarities and patterns.

TEACHING VERSUS COACHING

To develop employees' skills, you must first decide whether to teach or coach. Are you working with an inexperienced colleague or one who requires immediate improvement? If so, you'll want to teach, which means showing or telling her what to do. Otherwise, you're probably better off coaching—asking questions that prompt her to think and solve problems on her own. That way, your employee will gain the independence and confidence she needs to grow, whether she's trying to achieve greater mastery in her role or take on new responsibilities.

Approach:	Used for:	Example:
Teaching: a *directive* approach	Instructing	Having an employee shadow you on a task or project, such as a joint sales call, so that she can learn by observing you
	Providing answers	Explaining the business strategy to a new hire
Coaching: a *supportive* approach	Encouraging independence	Allowing someone to learn on the job, even if it means risking mistakes
	Serving as a resource	Providing helpful contacts so that your employee can learn from others, not just you

Adapted from *Harvard Business Essentials: Coaching and Mentoring* (Harvard Business School Press, 2004)

That exercise helped one manager recognize her tendency to jump right into action rather than spend time defining and aligning processes. She noticed how impatient she became when team members kept pulling conversations back to "process" instead of "just getting the work done." When she asked them for candid feedback on this, they explained that her impatience actually slowed them down (the last thing she wanted to do) because they often had to loop back to clarify expectations with her. So her impact—as well as her team's—didn't match her intent. She met her employees halfway by doing a better job of clarifying expectations up front. She also encouraged them to make more adjustments on the fly so they wouldn't get paralyzed by planning and slavish adherence to process. As the general level of impatience and frustration dropped, the group began to operate more efficiently and enjoyed the work more.

Matching people's skills with big-picture needs

As a coach to your employees, you're not just helping them grow for their own sake—noble as that is. You're also boosting their ability to support the company's mission and goals. By explicitly connecting their skills with big-picture needs, you'll give them a sense of purpose and belonging, which will motivate them to grow. If you explain how improving their communication skills will make the team more efficient, for example, or increase sales to clients, they'll be more likely to take their development in that area as seriously as you do.

How can you get better at connecting the dots between their skills and the organization's needs? There's no magic here—again, you'll get a wealth of information simply by asking. Where do they feel their skills are best used? What excites them about their work? What areas do they struggle with? What would they like to do more of? Less of? How do they see all that fitting into the organization's objectives? (For more on channeling employees' passions and strengths, see chapter 2, "Set the Stage to Stimulate Growth.")

Make it clear that you're looking out for their interests as well as the company's. They'll be eager to help you figure out how they can best serve the organization—and how the organization (and you) can best serve them.

Developing a growth mind-set means you're learning right along with your employees. The more coaching practice you get, the sharper your skills will become—but give yourself a running start by favoring inquiry over advocacy. Ask questions about others' intent, your own biases, and individuals' place in the big picture. And resist the temptation to coach by explaining how *you* do things. With prompting, not lecturing, your employees will discover solutions of their own and make greater, more lasting progress toward their developmental goals.

Candice Frankovelgia is a coaching portfolio manager and a senior faculty member at the Center for Creative Leadership.

Chapter 2
Set the Stage to Stimulate Growth

by Edward M. Hallowell, MD

Editor's note: Before you begin coaching your employees, set the stage for success. Make sure they're doing the right jobs to begin with, they feel connected to their work and to one another, they're receptive, and they're capable of mastering the skills and tasks their roles require. Using basic principles from brain science, you can address each of those issues and help people achieve peak performance.

The brain is remarkably *plastic*: It grows and adapts throughout life.

That means you're never stuck with who you are or who your employees are. We used to think only young

Adapted from *Shine: Using Brain Science to Get the Best from Your People* (product #9238), by Edward M. Hallowell, MD, Harvard Business Review Press, 2011 brains could change and develop. We now know that adult brains do, too. We can all get smarter and wiser and happier. The conventional, dreary wisdom that people can't change is scientifically incorrect.

We've also discovered many of the forces that make the brain change for better or worse. For example, challenging a person in an area where she is skilled makes her brain grow, much like a muscle. But overwhelming her with more than she can cope with is bad for her brain. Instilling confidence in someone leads to improved performance. But an atmosphere of chronic fear disables the brain and makes performance worse.

So, what about the guy down the hall who keeps failing in his role? With proper care, he can learn to perform at higher levels—he can continue to grow for decades. And you, as his manager, can help him do so.

Achieving Peak Performance

Drawing on what we know about neuroplasticity, I've outlined a practical plan for achieving peak performance. By *peak performance,* I don't mean taking on every task and embracing every opportunity. When people try to do more than they can handle, they fall short. Instead, I'm talking about *consistent excellence, with improvement over time at a specific task or set of tasks.*

How can people pull that off? By following these five steps, with your guidance and support.

Step 1: Select

Before your employees do anything, it's important to figure out what they *should* do. Help them achieve peak performance by selecting tasks (1) that they are good at; (2) that they like to do; and (3) that add value to the project or organization. The intersection of those three elements creates the magical field in which consistent excellence can happen.

This first step influences everything that follows, yet it is often overlooked. Millions of employees underachieve simply because they stumbled into the wrong job and never got out of it. It is critical that you know your employees well enough to help them get into the right slots in the organization.

Consider Mary Ann, a customer service associate at a large financial services firm. After five years of answering customer calls, there wasn't a problem she hadn't heard or solved. Even so, she never felt 100% comfortable in her role. She got flustered when customers became irritated, and she dreaded fielding the calls. As a result, she took a bit longer than she should answering calls in the queue, which meant that she served fewer customers. Customer reviews were OK but not great. In general, Mary Ann seemed to lack enthusiasm, to merely go through the motions.

One night, while chatting with her at a company-sponsored happy hour, her manager discovered that Mary Ann trained volunteers at a local nonprofit every weekend. She loved the work and looked forward to it. What she enjoyed most was helping the young volunteers develop their skills.

The next day, the manager reassigned Mary Ann. Rather than taking calls, she became responsible for training new customer service associates. Suddenly Mary Ann started to thrive. She was excited to come to work and brimming with new ideas for training associates and improving customer service. Younger associates began to look up to her. The number of calls answered by the department increased; customer reviews improved.

With her manager's assistance, Mary Ann found the right match for herself in the organization. She took on the kind of work she enjoyed most, used skills that set her apart from others, and began adding more value to the organization—all of which allowed her to deliver peak performance.

As Mary Ann's manager did, look for the telltale signs of a wrong fit: You can tell that someone is not in the right role if he never gets excited about his job, for example, or if he chronically complains. This doesn't mean he's dull or that the line of work he's in is intrinsically dull—just that he's not assigned to the right tasks.

Investigate your employees' skills and interests so that you can deploy people to their (and your) best advantage. How? By using the most powerful assessment tool ever invented: the one-on-one conversation.

It astonishes me how few managers do this. Clients often tell me, "No one has ever asked me what I like to do or what I do best." They say they don't volunteer that information because they don't want to make waves. While I always encourage them to speak up anyway—it is in everyone's best interest—it's simpler if managers take the initiative.

A structured interview (see the sidebar at the end of this chapter) can help you unearth your direct reports' strengths and passions. Ask each employee to take a few days to think carefully about their replies to each question and write down their answers. Then have a conversation to review the answers in person.

As you talk face-to-face, you'll develop understanding and trust. You'll also be able to ask follow-up questions and give employees the wonderful—and in some organizations, rare—experience of feeling heard. That alone will boost their motivation and performance.

Step 2: Connect

People who feel connected to others, to their tasks, and to the organization's mission perform at the highest levels. They're loyal, excited to contribute, and even willing to make sacrifices to preserve that sense of attachment. As a manager, you can foster it by creating an environment where it's safe for people to be themselves and forge ties. You'll inspire them to do far more than they thought they could.

The modern workplace tends to leave people *disconnected*—emotionally alone, isolated, exhausted, anxious, and afraid—with no idea how they got that way or what to do about it. Often, they're too mentally overloaded or too stressed to converse and connect. This kind of disengagement short-circuits performance more quickly than anything else.

One of the greatest disconnectors is fear. People may fear disapproval, a poor result, criticism, looking stupid, going beyond their comfort zone, or making others look bad. Whatever the cause, if they're afraid, they underachieve.

Here again, brain science shows us why. As fear mounts, the brain's deep centers take over. Areas like the amygdala, the hypothalamus, and the locus coeruleus light up. Higher cortical thinking—concocting new ideas, seeing shades of gray—ceases because the brain must devote its full attention to the perceived threat. If there were a saber-toothed tiger about to jump out at you, this would be good. You would not want to be concocting new ideas and seeing shades of gray. You'd want to be fleeing or killing the tiger. But a saber-toothed manager—or, more generally, a culture of fear at work—can elicit the same response. Excessive fear renders peak performance neurologically impossible.

So make it a priority to promote positive connections for employees—and to rein in fear.

As human beings, we are wired to connect. When we see another person in distress, for example, our "mirror neurons" create an imagined version of that distress within us. This is the biological basis for empathy, and it is common to us all.

Why, then, do so many people struggle to connect with others? We're all too busy. We do not spend enough time together, face-to-face. We overrely on electronic connections and so don't develop the trust required for candid exchanges. But you can help your employees overcome those forces. Try the following techniques:

1. **Noticing and acknowledging your employees.**
    People feel good when they are acknowledged—
    and bad when they're not. You do not need to
    have deep conversations to promote connection.
    Just saying hi or even smiling works wonders.
    To walk past someone as if that person were not

there—which happens *all the time*—is a surefire disconnector.

2. **Allowing for idiosyncrasies and peccadilloes.** Encourage your employees to be who they are. We're all a little strange. When you are relaxed about yourself as a manager, you give others permission to be the same.

3. **Encouraging conversation.** Agree as a group not to send e-mails without first considering whether it's better to communicate in person or over the phone. And never use e-mail to work out emotionally laden issues. Simple changes like these will reset people's attentional systems. Employees will become less ravenous for distraction and less likely to look to e-mails or text messages for a "fix." They'll train their brains to wait while they do more important work. And they will be more likely to communicate with others in person, which fosters connection.

4. **Encouraging breaks.** When you can see that people are starting to feel stressed, urge them to stop what they're doing. Even switching to something else can help. Many "disconnecting" episodes—flare-ups, arguments, and the like— occur as a direct result of stress.

5. **Offering food and drink.** Food is a symbolic form of nurturing. Stock up on fruits, nuts, and bottles of sparkling water.

6. **Fostering impromptu get-togethers.** Planned parties are fine, but they are often command performances and can feel stilted. Impromptu gatherings—grabbing lunch, going out for coffee, catching a ball game after work—all promote connectedness.

Step 3: Play

Not enough managers recognize the importance of *play* in catalyzing peak performance. By play, I mean *any activity that involves imagination.* So defined, it constitutes the most advanced, productive activity the human brain can engage in. When workers seem dull or apathetic, it is usually because they are not engaged in imaginative, creative problem solving.

By valuing and promoting play, you can transform your employees' performance. Here are some ways to encourage people to leap from the humdrum to the exceptional:

1. **Ask open-ended questions.** The Socratic method remains one of the best ways to teach. Instead of giving answers, ask questions that engage the imagination, invite people to brainstorm and reflect, and help them make discoveries. For example:

   - What can we learn from what just happened?

   - Where did we go wrong?

   - What are we doing right?

   - What else could we do?

- What changes could we make to the prototype?

- Why are we spending so much time on this topic?

- What are we avoiding?

2. **Model a questioning attitude.** Show people that it is safe to disagree with the party line and with the boss—that it is in fact *good* to bring up opposing points of view. You need to model this. Your employees aren't likely to initiate such behavior on their own.

3. **Decorate and arrange your workspace with an eye toward facilitating play.** You might choose lively color schemes, for example, or rearrange work areas to increase opportunities for interaction, as the Atlanta Housing Authority did when it revamped its cubicle system. It lowered cubicle walls to improve sight lines between employees and set up "teaming tables" where employees could conveniently share ideas and their work.

4. **Try what organic chemists call "retrograde synthesis."** In chemistry, you work backward from the molecule you are trying to synthesize. You can use the same approach to jump-start play and creativity. Simply envision your goal and work your way back, step-by-step, until you get to where you are now.

Step 4: Grapple and Grow

This step is about mastering challenging tasks that *matter.* People who do this feel a sense of well-being and accomplishment—and their success makes them want to work even harder.

But before you ask more of people, consider the following:

- Are they operating at the intersection of what they like, what they're good at, and what adds value to the organization?

- Do they feel safe at work, comfortable enough to be candid and open, connected enough to look forward to coming in?

- Are they imaginatively engaged with their work?

Only when you can say yes to all those questions— that is, after you've helped people select, connect, and play—will hard work lead to growth. Otherwise it leads to stress, frustration, mistakes, depression, absenteeism, and inferior performance. Just as achieving mastery can instill confidence and motivation, failing to make progress can damage self-esteem and *de*motivate people.

So be on the lookout for frustration or a lack of progress. When you see a logjam, break it by redirecting employees to other tasks or providing coaching to help them overcome obstacles. And encourage people to ask for help when they need it. Let them know it is not only OK but desirable to do so.

Step 5: Shine

As your employees work hard and advance, they'll gain recognition—which affirms the value of what they've accomplished. Help them shine by praising and rewarding them for a job well executed. People who shine are motivated. They feel connected and extremely loyal to the team, the group, and the organization. They want to keep shining, and they want to help others shine, too.

Edward M. Hallowell, MD, a psychiatrist, served as an instructor at Harvard Medical School for 20 years. He is the director of the Hallowell Centers in New York City, San Francisco, and Sudbury, Massachusetts.

STRUCTURED INTERVIEW:
ARE YOUR EMPLOYEES DOING THE RIGHT TASKS?

Give this questionnaire to your direct reports. Lay out the ground rules and let everyone know exactly how the information will be used, who will have access to it, and where it will be stored. Only after you've dispelled people's fears will they open up and give you useful information.

This questionnaire is a tool for putting what you already know about yourself into words. As you fill it out, you will be generating what amounts to a neuropsychological assessment—not the kind that a doctor would conduct, but one that is in many ways more useful.

(*continued*)

STRUCTURED INTERVIEW:
ARE YOUR EMPLOYEES DOING THE RIGHT TASKS?

(*continued*)

Once you have answered these questions, you and your manager will be better able to find the right tasks for you at work because you will have a clearer idea of what your skills and preferences are, how you work best in the organization, and under what conditions you feel most comfortable and motivated.

1. What are you best at doing? (Can you think of ways to incorporate more of what you do best into your job?)

2. What do you most like to do? (This is not always the same as what you do best. Unless it is illegal or bad for you, you ought to preserve sizable chunks of time for what you most like to do.)

3. What do you wish you were better at? (This may be a skill you can develop through coaching or a task you should delegate.)

4. What talents do you have that you haven't developed? (Don't say "none." Everyone has bundles of them. Pick a few. Just because you name them doesn't mean you have to develop them.)

5. What skills are you most proud of? (This may reflect obstacles you have overcome.)

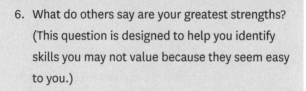

6. What do others say are your greatest strengths? (This question is designed to help you identify skills you may not value because they seem easy to you.)

7. What have you gotten better at that you used to be bad at? (This gives you an idea of where putting in additional effort can pay off.)

8. What are you just not getting better at, no matter how hard you try? (This tells you where you shouldn't waste more time.)

9. What do you most dislike doing? (Your answer here suggests what tasks you might want to delegate or hire out.)

10. The lack of which skills most gets in your way? (If you lack a skill required in your current job and you can't delegate it, then that is getting in your way. Your answer to this question might lead you to take a course, read a book, or work with a coach.)

11. What sorts of people do you work best and worst with? (Do you hate to work with highly organized analytic types, or do you love it? Do creative types drive you crazy, or do you work well with them? Make up your own categories.)

(continued)

STRUCTURED INTERVIEW:
ARE YOUR EMPLOYEES DOING THE RIGHT TASKS?

(*continued*)

12. What sort of organizational culture brings out the best in you? (It's amazing how many people won't leave a culture they are hideously unsuited to work in.)

13. What were you doing when you were happiest in your work life? (Could you find a way to incorporate that into what you're doing now?)

14. What regrets do you have about how you have run your career? (Could you make any changes based on those regrets?)

15. What are your most cherished hopes for the future, workwise? (What stands in the way of realizing those hopes?)

16. What are you most proud of in your work life? (Your answer here is another tip-off as to what you should be doing.)

17. What one lesson about managing a career would you pass along to the next generation? (This question is another way of getting at your thoughts on what you have done, what's worked, and what hasn't.)

18. What was the most important work-related lesson you learned from your parents? (As you reflect on this, you will get an idea of how attitudes are passed from generation to generation and shape how your mind works.)

19. What lesson did the best boss you ever had teach you about yourself? (Other people often know us better than we do.)

20. How could your time be better used in your current job to add value to the organization? (Your answer here gives your manager valuable input he or she may never have asked for.)

Adapted from the "Hallowell Self-Report Job-Fit Scale" in *Shine*

Chapter 3
Earn Your Employees' Trust

by Jim Dougherty

When I took over as CEO of Intralinks, a company that provides secure Web-based electronic deal rooms, the company was hemorrhaging so much cash that its survival was at stake. The service was going down three times per week; we were in violation of the contract with our largest client; our chief administrative officer had just been demoted, and so on.

So what did I do on my first day? I spent more than four hours listening to client support calls at the call center. I shared headsets with many of the team, moving from desk to desk to speak to the reps. To say they were surprised is an understatement: Many CEOs never visit the call center, and virtually none do it on their first afternoon on the job.

I made this my priority in part because I wanted to gain the trust of my team. I knew we had to make radical changes to behaviors, expectations, and attitudes. There was no time to be subtle. I needed to show I was different, that things were going to be different, and I needed to establish trust as quickly as possible.

As I've led various companies over the years, one of the most valuable lessons I've learned is that establishing trust is the top priority. Whether you are taking over a small department, an entire division, a company, or even a Boy Scout troop, the first thing you must get is the trust of the members. When asked, most leaders will agree to this notion, but few do anything to act on it.

Without trust, employees won't level with you; at best, you'll learn either untruths or partial truths about how they see themselves and their roles within the organization. They won't tell you what their own goals are, or their weaknesses, or how they want to grow—critical information if you're going to help them develop within the organization. Sometimes employees will go out of their way to hoard and distort the truth, especially if they fear that you will throw them under the bus if they make a mistake—or if *you* make a mistake. And if you don't have their trust, it will also make it harder for them to hear and react constructively to your feedback—whether positive or corrective—about the changes you want them to make. Finally, without trust, it is very unlikely that you as a leader will learn the truth about what is really going on in your organization and in the marketplace.

As you learn more about your direct reports, exchanging information about your personal lives is a way to build trust as well, but you don't want to be too invasive. That line is different for every person, and you'll need to feel it out. I usually start by asking where someone is from: then he'll share as much as he feels is appropriate. You should reciprocate with information about yourself.

Note that you need to have a legitimate interest in what is going on in his life. Don't fake it. For example, commit to memory how old his children are. I also keep a Word document for each of my employees to remind me about the things they've told me so that I'll remember about little Jimmy's recital or Laila's soccer game and can ask about how they went.

Building Trust Through Behaviors

Listening to your employees and acting on what you hear are one part of how you'll gain their trust, but your day-to-day behaviors also affect how much they believe you're authentically interested in their growth and development.

Here are some tips.

- **Give credit where credit's due.** In any situation in which you're describing your team's accomplishments, think and say "we" rather than "I." If one of your direct reports contributed to a project, go out of your way to credit her, especially as the project is presented to a wider group or to management levels higher than yours. This is a great way to show your employees that taking growth assignments will bring them rewards.

- **Set an example.** Your team members see everything you do. If you expect them to grow in certain ways, take feedback in certain ways, or shift their behavior in certain ways, you need to model those things for them. If you practice what you preach, they'll take you at your word on other things.

- **Take one for the team.** Accepting an occasional tedious assignment, or taking one off the plate of one of your team members—especially if it means that he's able to attend a concert or game he thought he'd have to miss—goes a long way toward showing your reports that you're on their side. It also models selfless behavior for them: They'll be more willing to take on the next assignment you delegate or help out when a colleague is in the same predicament.

- **Be transparent with tough decisions and feedback.** Just because you want to show you're on their side doesn't mean tough decisions will favor your team's whims or wishes or that you won't sometimes have strong constructive feedback. (And being known as a pushover doesn't help you become trusted.) When you have to convey tough news, be clear and transparent, and provide as much explanation as you can. Be open to questions and feedback.

By the end of my first year on the job we'd signed 150 new long-term contracts (up from zero), revenue was up by almost 600%, our burn rate was cut by 75%, and we'd positioned ourselves to raise a $50 million round of financing a few months later in the depth of the dot-com winter.

None of this could have happened without the team's amazing growth over the course of that year, and that couldn't have happened if team members didn't trust me when I pushed them, prodded them, and demanded the world of them. New leaders must remember that the key to success lies in the growth of their team. Creating a trusting, honest dialogue with these key personnel should be every new leader's top priority.

———————

Jim Dougherty, a veteran software CEO and entrepreneur, is a senior lecturer at MIT Sloan School of Management.

Section 2
Coaching Your Employees

Chapter 4
Holding a Coaching Session

by Amy Jen Su

Coaching sessions are conversations between you and your employee in which you identify areas for growth, create development plans, perform exercises, and check in on progress. A coaching session can kick off a specific development process around a particular skill or behavior as needed; you can then hold further sessions to follow up and monitor progress. A coaching session can also be a regular, more general conversation about the employee's growth.

Coaching sessions are distinct from other types of conversations you may already be having with your employees, such as performance reviews or regular check-ins. Table 4–1 compares and contrasts the focus and time frames for each of these; you'll notice that of these three

TABLE 4-1

Types of direct report meetings

Meeting type	Time horizon	Focus
Performance review	Annual; retrospective	Assess performance of the employee retrospectively over a given time period against a set of objectives related to current job responsibilities. Formal.
One-on-one meeting	Typically weekly or biweekly; current	Discuss existing business projects, work plans, and objectives related to current job responsibilities. Informal.
Coaching sessions	Generally once per month; retrospective, current, and prospective	Discuss development and growth. Addresses both recent and current performance and future potential. Can be formal or informal.

types of conversations, the coaching session is the one that has the broadest time horizon and also looks the farthest forward to examine, plan, and work toward your direct report's future.

Coaching sessions typically range from 30 minutes to an hour, but they do not have to be long to be successful. In fact, research from the Corporate Executive Board shows that there is "no connection between time . . . and effectiveness at development."[1] Instead of adding more coaching time to your already full load as a manager, make the most of each session. You can do so by asking the right questions and engaging in dialogue to increase your direct report's awareness of her own choices, actions, and behaviors, along with their impact—as well as gain her buy in for the development plan.

Agree to Outcomes at the Start

As a first step in your coaching session, work together with your direct report to define what you're looking to achieve. Is there a particular skill she has been working on? A question she has about how to handle a particular colleague or type of assignment? A long-term goal she wants to work toward? And what kind of progress can you expect to make in your time together today?

Encourage your employee to take part in identifying a clear scope for the session by directly asking her what *she* hopes to achieve and what she wants to make sure to get to. You can offer ideas for further shaping the agenda based on your previous observations, but in most cases you'll want to start your coaching session by asking your direct report to share her own impressions. This might catch her off guard; more likely she will expect you to set the agenda. But by opening your session with a question, you begin as you'll hope to continue: with your employee talking, you listening, and with both of you then building solutions together.

There are many types of coaching sessions, but here are three of the most popular:

- **Long-term development help.** For example, "I want to increase my comfort around senior management and get better at presenting to this audience." This type of coaching focuses on a goal that takes time and practice, anywhere from six months to a year, with follow-up coaching sessions at least once per month. To keep focused on the development plan and to take the opportunity to build successively on the learning from each session, schedule these follow-ups in advance.

- **Debrief on an event or project.** For example, "The meeting with the other team did not go as well as planned. I would like to review what happened and determine what I could do differently next time." This type focuses on learning from recent events to identify new ideas, skills, and ways of handling similar situations in the future. This type of meeting often occurs in a follow-up coaching session embedded in long-term development help, but it may also be purely episodic: a chance to learn from a onetime mistake or an opportunity to praise and encourage a productive behavior.

- **Short-term problem solving.** For example, "Our colleague in another division has been making multiple requests with unreasonable deadlines. I would like your help on how to better respond and prioritize these." This is a highly focused coaching session: Your employee has something specific she needs help with in real time. It requires getting to the heart of the matter so that she leaves the session with actionable tasks she can use to address the problem immediately. Sometimes a short-term problem may help uncover a longer-term development need, but that is not always the case. These types of problems may come up in your regular one-on-one meetings as you delve into a project or other day-to-day work. Recognize these as opportunities to put on your coaching hat; many managers miss them.

Setting the explicit goals of your coaching session in this way allows you to plan how to proceed: what kinds of questions to ask and how to frame a solution.

Build a Baseline Understanding of the Issues

Once you understand what kind of coaching your direct report is looking for, you will probably feel tempted to "fix the problem" immediately—to share your wisdom about the topic, give her the advice you think she needs, or carefully explain your point of view about why things didn't go well. But don't do it! This is the place where coaching most often goes wrong.

Instead, at this stage you need to get more information to create a clear baseline understanding of the situation: Your employee very likely still knows more about it than you do. To help her develop effectively, you need to learn more about her point of view of the situation and any related situations in the past, and her level of development with the skill involved. Could she be struggling because she has an outdated mind-set that is repeatedly getting in the way? Does she lack a certain skill? Have her emotions been triggered by something in a way that is holding her back? Is she not preparing as well as she could? Collecting background information is critical to making an assessment of the root causes of your employee's challenge and thus identifying an effective development path.

Tell your employee that you would like to learn more about the situation and ask her questions that can help you understand her perspective. For example, for the employee with the long-term goal of becoming more comfortable around senior management, ask questions that probe her past experiences and their effects on her and others, as well as her current processes. These questions might include:

- How would you describe your current level of comfort around our senior team?

- When you have presented to this audience in the past, how would you describe your impact?

- How do you prepare for these interactions now?

- When have you been effective in these types of interactions? Ineffective?

- What was different or similar about the meetings when you were effective versus those when you weren't?

For an employee who is many coaching sessions in, a focused debrief of a particular event or project is more appropriate. In this case you can home in more closely on the details.

- How did the presentation you gave to this group go on Friday?

- How would you describe the impact you had?

- What worked well? What didn't?

Or, for an employee with a short-term problem, ask questions that give you a more concrete sense of the issue and its impact.

- Tell me more about the situation. What are the requests being made, and what are the deadlines involved?

- Which of these are tied to our highest department priorities?

- What trade-offs will we have to make in order to meet the high-priority requests?

Keep your questions open-ended; starting your questions with the words *what*, *how*, or *tell me more* tends to draw out an answer, whereas starting with *why* or asking a closed-ended question (in which the answer is a simple yes or no) can make the employee defensive. In answering your skillfully worded questions, your employee may already begin identifying some root causes and solutions she didn't see before. This self-awareness will increase her buy in for any actions or development plan that will come out of the session.

Hold Up the Mirror, Reframe, and Practice New Skills

Once you have a stronger understanding of the situation, it may again be tempting to simply offer a solution or hand down a piece of advice. Instead, now aim for an open, robust two-way dialogue in which you help the employee herself understand possible new choices, new strategies, or new skills she could develop. Here are several tactics for creating a productive dialogue:

- **Hold up the mirror.** What did you hear as your employee spoke that particularly struck you? Offer her a reflection that redescribes the situation she has outlined with your own perspective, and then ask for her response to that reflection. For example, you might say, "Based on what you have shared, it seems that two things may be creating your discomfort with senior management. First, a mind-set around positional authority may be leading you to be more deferential than necessary. Second, there may be an opportunity to increase your skill in preparing for these types of interactions to raise your comfort level. Do those things resonate?"

- **Frame or reframe the situation.** Help her see the situation differently. "Could I offer you a new way of thinking about the situation? Perhaps we could explore a broader range of what appropriate respect for senior management could look like. The frame you currently have focuses your attention on the differences in your age and experience with these individuals, which may be making you more nervous and tentative. Instead, consider what it would mean to focus on the shared conviction you feel for what we need to do for the business. As you hear me say these things, what resonates and what doesn't?"

- **Practice or role-play.** A coaching session is a great time to practice new skills or a new mind-set with your employee. In our example, you and your employee might role-play an upcoming interaction with senior management. You'll get to observe her behavior and offer real-time guidance about the way certain behaviors can be perceived. In addition to role-playing, you could review an ideal example of the type of behavior or skill you are working on. For example, review a presentation that has worked well for senior management; you could go over it together and discuss why this one was effective. You can also review your direct report's current processes together: She could show you how she prepares for these meetings now, and you can fine-tune her preparation techniques together.

As you offer assessments, introduce possible new frames, and practice exercises, continue to check in with your employee to make sure that what you are saying and doing is resonating for her. If not, take the opportunity to ask more questions and find out more about the situation before proceeding. The observations, suggestions, and practices that you offer are the core of your coaching session, but to be effective they need to be tailored to her particular situation.

Ensure an Actionable and Practical Close

As you near the end of the coaching session, ask your employee to articulate what she's learned and what her action items are, saying something like, "As we get to the last ten minutes here of our session, what are the top two or three things you are taking away from our conversation?" Your employee may highlight a-ha's that particularly struck her, or new ways of seeing things that have helped her think differently about her situation. Or she may share the things she is excited to practice or do differently. Having your direct report summarize her gains—rather than doing it yourself—helps with her buy in; it also allows you to sense what she's heard and what she might yet have to learn.

Consider the coaching session as a kickoff for the employee's actual development: The rubber will hit the road once she puts what she's learned to use. While you're both still in the room, agree on when to check in again, and identify any tasks to be completed before then. In this example, you and your employee might agree to meet again in a month; in the meantime she will get ready for another senior-level meeting using the preparation techniques you worked on together in the coaching session.

Continue to demonstrate openness and support as your time together draws to a close, asking questions like, "Is there anything else that you hoped we would get to today? Come by between now and our next session on this if you have questions or need to discuss something."

Over time, by asking so many questions of your employee as part of the coaching session, you will also help develop her own ability to coach herself—asking herself the questions that you've often teed up for her—so that she can continue to grow even without you by her side.

Amy Jen Su is managing partner and cofounder of Paravis Partners, an executive coaching and training firm. She is an executive coach and speaker on issues of leadership presence, communication excellence, and executive endurance—factors critical to a leader's performance success. She is coauthor with Muriel Maignan Wilkins of *Own the Room: Discover Your Signature Voice to Master Your Leadership Presence* (Harvard Business Review Press, 2013).

NOTE

1. Corporate Leadership Council Learning and Development, Manager-Led Development Effectiveness Survey, available at https://clc.executiveboard.com/Public/PDF/CLC_LD_Program_Brochure.pdf.

Chapter 5
Following Up After a Coaching Session

by Pam Krulitz and Nina Bowman

It is often said that the real work of coaching happens *after* a coaching session. That's when you and your direct report actually put your conversation into practice, after all. But as a manager, how do you make sure to follow up appropriately? And how do you know whether your coaching is working?

Align Expectations for Follow-Up

After a coaching meeting, your direct report can quickly become aware of how difficult it is to balance new coaching commitments with the hectic demands of normal day-to-day work. To keep the process on track, you need to work with him in advance to set up a thoughtful approach for maintaining momentum between sessions.

While still in the coaching meeting itself, set clear agreements about how you will move forward. Address the following.

- **Action items.** Agree on the specific actions that you and your direct report will take between sessions. For example, if he is working on developing peer relationships, he may agree to have lunch with some of those peers before your next meeting. He may agree to hold a difficult conversation with a direct report whom he's been avoiding. Coaching can provide an excellent accountability mechanism to hold your employees to task for the things they've said they want to do to develop—but only if you clearly define those actions and their deadlines up front.

- **Feedback.** Provide feedback after your initial coaching session either in the moment or, more likely, in additional formal coaching sessions. Agreeing on how you will proceed and being clear about the frequency of your involvement between sessions will prevent your direct reports from being unnecessarily stressed or frustrated by well-intentioned check-ins. You will also want to decide whether others in the organization will play a role in offering feedback throughout the coaching process. For example, a direct report who is struggling with speaking up in group settings may want to include a peer who can observe him in meetings and provide informal feedback.

- **Resource needs.** Ask your employee what tools or support may be helpful. He may need specific learning resources, such as articles, books, assessments, or training programs. He may also need you to connect him with others in the organization for mentoring, or to have him shadow you in meetings. Understanding his needs will let you know which resources you will need to identify and gather between coaching meetings.

As you discuss these items, ask your employee about his preferences. Don't just impose your way of doing things.

Capture what you've agreed upon after each meeting. Depending on the tools available and the process followed in your organization, you may ask your direct report to complete a coaching plan template or document the goals he's agreed to in a system that captures development plans. Or you may simply have him send a follow-up e-mail documenting your agreements and expectations. Table 5–1 shows an example of a coaching action plan.

Check In on Your Direct Report

With your expectations aligned, after each coaching session you can continue to support your employee's development in the following ways.

- **Follow up on agreements.** Because we naturally tend to focus on what's in front of us or what's due next, the longer-term agreements made in your coaching conversation can easily fall by the

TABLE 5-1

Goals and action plan

Goals *What skills or competencies do I want to develop?*	Action steps *What do I need to do to develop in these areas?*	Measures of success *What will be the impact if I am successful:* *– On myself?* *– On my colleagues?* *– On my results?*
1. I want to better focus on my long-term priorities.	• Delegate more responsibility to team members and do so clearly, making them the point of contact to outside groups for their areas of responsibility. • Set up regular, one-on-one time with each team member to minimize responding to questions and issues throughout the day. • Put my top 3 goals for the month on my computer as my screen saver. • Take 15 minutes each morning to plan for the day, and make sure enough time is allocated toward my long-term priorities. • When I'm asked to do something, take a deep breath, reflect on the need behind the request, and consider my options rather than saying yes immediately. • Read David Allen's *Getting Things Done* and the HBR article "Manage Your Energy, Not Your Time" for additional ideas.	• I'll feel less frazzled when I arrive in the morning and when I'm heading home in the evening. • My team will feel more ownership for their areas of responsibility and will not ask as many questions. • I'll be able to check off some of my longer-term goals.

| 2. I want to be more clear and succinct in my communications. | • Before each meeting I attend, jot down the two or three points that I want to make or ideas I have about the topic.
• Before sending an e-mail or speaking in a meeting, consider the most important message I want to send and focus on that, providing additional context only if it is relevant to my audience.
• Reread each e-mail before sending to check for clear, strong, actionable tone and message.
• Reduce use of qualifiers such as "I think . . . ," "I'm not sure but . . . ," "you know . . ."
• Make strong requests: what I need, when I need it by, and whom I need it from.
• Read Amy Jen Su and Muriel Maignan Wilkins's *Own the Room: Discover Your Signature Voice to Master Your Leadership Presence.* | • My voice and opinions will be heard and considered more often.
• I'll feel more confident in my contribution and value.
• My team will be less confused and I'll get fewer e-mail replies asking for explanations. |

Source: ©Isis Associates 2004–2013.

wayside. If you don't follow up on those agreements, however, your direct report is less likely
to take them seriously. Periodically reviewing
the written plan will hold everyone accountable:
You'll be more likely to stick to the agreed-upon
check-in dates, provide your employee with the
resources such as the articles and books you identified, and follow up with engaging others in his
development.

- **Observe signs of growth.** Continually assess how
  your direct report is doing by keeping an eye on
  his performance, however informally. Are you
  seeing signs of progress in his behavior, his relationships, his attitude, or his results? Are others
  speaking about him differently? For example, if he
  is working on being a better listener in meetings,
  you may choose to carefully observe him in a few
  gatherings and jot down your own thoughts.

- **Check in directly.** Employees can get stuck between sessions; a new behavior may not work as
  hoped, or they may get frustrated with the ups and
  downs of the learning process. A simple check-
  in can get them unstuck and moving forward
  again. Initiate these as you've planned, but also
  consider instituting an open-door policy that
  encourages your direct reports to come to you if
  they have questions. During these check-ins, ask
  your employee about how things are changing and
  whether he himself is seeing any signs of development. Encourage him to jot down things that he's

noticing or learning, and use this material as the basis for your next formal coaching meeting.

- **Communicate impact.** As you see your direct report begin to change and grow, communicate the impact of his growth to him explicitly: It may be harder for him to see. What impact is coaching making on him as an individual? Is he being included in more strategic discussions? What is the impact on your group or division? Has that group been able to achieve more of its goals? What is the impact on the organization? Helping your employee understand the full effect of the changes that he is working hard to achieve can increase his motivation and serve as a reminder that the coaching you are providing serves both him *and* the organization.

- **Focus on the relationship.** As you work with your direct report, continue to foster an environment of openness and willingness to learn. If you sense a shift in the relationship, a decline in trust, or hesitation toward openness, it may be time to check in explicitly on what he is thinking and feeling after your conversations.

In the meantime, stay attuned to the following signs that the coaching process may be going off track, and intervene early.

- Your direct report comes to coaching meetings without having completed agreed-upon assignments or practices.

- Your direct report blames others for his failures as he tries new things, or he doesn't feel comfortable talking about both successes and failures.

- Your direct report doesn't demonstrate ownership of the coaching process by pushing back on you when appropriate or suggesting new ideas and methods of his own.

What if you've been vigilant about thoughtful follow-up, but your direct report is still not progressing on a critical development need? You may need to enlist the help of someone outside your chain of command: A trusted colleague, a member of the HR team, or a professional external coach may have the objectivity, skills, and relationship to help your team member progress. Ultimately, you and your staff member may need to have a conversation about whether the role is the right fit for him.

Check In on Yourself

Although much of the follow-up process focuses on your direct report, the process also requires self-reflection on your part. As the manager and coach, you may want to ask yourself two questions.

1. **Am I meeting the needs of this employee?**
   The coaching process will look and feel different for each of your direct reports, and what works for one employee may not work for another. Approach the process with a trial-and-error mentality, and show openness in making ad-

justments along the way. Frequently ask your direct report what is working and what is not. Approaches that don't work for a person at one point in the process can succeed later, so if a new practice or exercise is proving difficult, you may need to either change the plan or encourage patience.

Meeting the needs of your employee during coaching may also mean having a conversation with him if you have differing views on how he is progressing. For example, he may share that he understood the lessons from the books you provided and found them useful, but if he doesn't appear to be putting the lessons into practice, it may mean that the approach isn't working despite his enthusiasm. It is important for you as the coach to use your own judgment in addition to the employee's feedback to determine whether his needs are really being met.

2. **Am I holding up my end of the bargain?**
   Assisting with the development of others can often expose your own strengths and weaknesses. For example, Lisa and her manager, Arya, agreed that Lisa needed to step up more and take more responsibility. However, when Lisa tried to take ownership of a particular project, Arya had trouble letting go, insisting on daily reviews of every detail. But when she took a moment to reflect on her role as a coach, Arya realized that developing Lisa on this particular goal would first mean

changing her own approach. Coaching often requires you as a manager to hold up a mirror to yourself to see whether you're unknowingly getting in the way of your direct report's progress or whether you're acting in ways that send mixed messages about your expectations.

Coaching can be a challenging and yet uplifting process for both direct report and manager as you watch your employee grow and add value to the organization in new and different ways. By incorporating a follow-up process that includes aligning expectations up front, checking in with your direct report and checking in with yourself, you can see, encourage, and spur that growth, with results that can be well worth the time and attention you invest.

Pam Krulitz is a managing partner with Paravis Partners and is on the faculty of the Georgetown University Leadership Coaching program. She coaches entrepreneurs, senior executives, and high potentials to support their growth as leaders and achievement of their business goals. **Nina Bowman** is a senior partner with Paravis Partners and provides executive coaching, training, and leadership development consulting services to senior executives.

Chapter 6
Giving Feedback That Sticks

by Ed Batista

Although coaching is primarily about asking questions rather than providing answers, your employees will want your candid feedback on their performance. I've been involved in thousands of feedback conversations with clients and students over the years, and again and again I've heard people say, "Just give it to me straight."

But that simple request can be difficult to fulfill. When you say "Can I give you some feedback?" to your employees, their heart rate and blood pressure are almost certain to increase, and they may experience other signs of stress as well. These are symptoms of a "threat response," also known as "fight-or-flight": a cascade of neurological and physiological events that impair the ability to process complex information and react thoughtfully. When people are in the grip of a threat response, they're less capable of absorbing and applying feedback.

You've probably observed this dynamic in feedback conversations with employees that didn't go as well as you'd hoped. Some people respond with explanations, defensiveness, or even hostility, while others minimize eye contact, cross their arms, hunch over, and generally look as if they'd rather be doing anything but talking to you. These fight-or-flight behaviors suggest that your feedback probably won't have the desired impact.

How do you avoid triggering a threat response—and deliver feedback your people can digest and use? These guidelines will help.

Cultivate the Relationship

We lay the foundations for effective feedback by building relationships with others over time. When people feel connected to us, even difficult conversations with them are less likely to trigger a threat response. Social psychologist John Gottman, a leading expert on building relationships, has found from his research that success in difficult conversations depends on what he calls "the quality of the friendship." Gottman cites several steps we can take to develop high-quality relationships:

- **Make the other person feel "known."** Making people aware that you see them as individuals— and not merely as employees—is a critical step in the process, but it need not be overly time-consuming. Several years ago a coaching client of mine who ran a midsize company felt that he was too distant from his employees but didn't have the time to take someone to lunch every day. His efficient compromise was to view every interaction, no matter how fleeting, as an opportunity to get to know that person a little better. He made a habit of asking employees one question about their work or their personal lives each time he encountered them. "Whenever I can, I connect," he told me. Although at times this slowed his progress through the office, the result was worth it.

- **Respond to even small bids for attention.** We seek attention from those around us not only in obvious ways but also through countless subtle "bids." As Gottman writes in *The Relationship Cure,* "A bid can be a question, a gesture, a look, a touch—any single expression that says, 'I want to feel connected to you.' A response to a bid is just that—a positive or negative answer to somebody's request for emotional connection." But many of us miss bids from our employees. That's because we're less observant of social cues from people over whom we wield authority, according to research by Dacher Keltner of the University of California, Berkeley, and others. To connect more effectively with employees, take stock of how much you notice—or miss—their efforts to gain your attention. And solicit feedback from peers, friends, and family members on your listening skills and how often you interrupt.

- **Regularly express appreciation.** As Gottman's research shows, the ratio of positive to negative interactions in a successful relationship is 5:1, even during periods of conflict. This ratio doesn't apply to a single conversation, and it doesn't mean that we're obligated to pay someone five compliments before we can offer critical feedback. But it does highlight the importance of providing positive feedback and expressing other forms of appreciation over time in order to strengthen the relationship. (See the sidebar "The Pitfalls of Positive Feedback.")

Manage Emotions

Although excessive negative feelings inhibit learning and communication, emotions play a vital role in feedback. They convey emphasis and let others know what we value. Emotional experiences stick with people, last longer in their memories, and are easier to recall. And extensive neuroscience research in recent decades makes clear that emotions are essential to our reasoning process: Strong emotions can pull us off course, but in general emotions support better decision making.

So while you'll want to avoid triggering a threat response, don't try to remove all emotion from your coaching. That can diminish the impact of your feedback and lead to a cycle of ineffective conversations. Instead, aim for a balance: Express *just enough* emotion to engage the other person but not so much that you provoke a hostile or defensive reaction, shut down the conversation, or damage the relationship.

The right amount of emotion depends on the issue you're addressing and varies from one relationship to another—and even from one day to the next. The key

THE PITFALLS OF POSITIVE FEEDBACK

Praise is supposed to make your employees feel good and motivate them, but often it does just the opposite. Here are three common problems and ways to avoid them:

1. ***People don't trust the praise.*** Before delivering unpleasant feedback to your direct reports, do you say something nice to soften the blow? Many of us do—and we unwittingly condition people to hear our positive feedback as a hollow preamble to the real message. Rather than feeling genuinely appreciated, they're waiting for the other shoe to drop. Though we've diminished our anxiety about bearing bad news, we haven't helped them receive it. We've actually undermined our ability to deliver any meaningful feedback, positive or negative.

   What to do: Instead of giving a spoonful of sugar before every dose of constructive criticism, lead off with your investment in the relationship and your reasons for having the conversation. For example: "It's important that we can be candid and direct with each other so we can work together effectively. I have some concerns for us to discuss, and I'm optimistic that we can resolve them."

2. ***People resent it.*** Managers also use positive feedback to overcome resistance to requests.

(continued)

THE PITFALLS OF POSITIVE FEEDBACK

(*continued*)

This age-old tactic can work in the moment but carries a long-term cost. It creates a sense of obligation, a "social debt" the recipient feels compelled to repay by acceding to your wishes. But if you train people to always expect requests after your praise, they'll eventually feel manipulated and resentful—and less inclined to help you out.

What to do: Motivate people over the long term by expanding your persuasive tool kit. As Jay Conger explains in his classic article "The Necessary Art of Persuasion" (HBR May–June 1998), you can gain lasting influence in four ways: establish credibility through expertise and work you've done in others' interests, frame goals around common ground and shared advantage, support your views with compelling data and examples, and connect emotionally with people so they'll be more receptive to your message.

3. **We praise the wrong things.** When aimed at the wrong targets, praise does more harm than good. As Stanford psychologist Carol Dweck notes in a January 2012 HBR IdeaCast interview, "The whole self-esteem movement taught us erroneously that praising intelligence, talent, and abilities would foster self-confidence and self-esteem, and everything great would follow. But we've found it

backfires. People who are praised for talent now worry about doing the next thing, about taking on the hard task, and not looking talented, tarnishing that reputation for brilliance. So they'll stick to their comfort zones and get really defensive when they hit setbacks."

What to do: Praise effort, not ability. Dweck suggests focusing on "the strategies, the doggedness and persistence, the grit and resilience" that people exhibit when facing challenges. And explain exactly what actions prompted your praise. If you're vague or generic, you'll fail to reinforce the desired behavior.

question is how responsive the other person will be to your emotions. A coaching client of mine who'd recently launched a company had some critical feedback for his cofounder, but previous conversations didn't have the desired effect. For the feedback to stick, my client needed to become fairly heated and more vocally and physically expressive. This worked because the two of them had a long-standing friendship. The cofounder didn't respond defensively—rather, the intensity got his attention. In contrast, when this same client of mine had some critical feedback for a subordinate, he reined in his emotions, modulated his expressiveness, and delivered the feedback in a matter-of-fact tone. The goal was to convey the importance of the issues without overwhelming the subordinate, and in this case my client's authority was sufficient on its own.

Of course, we may not know how another person will respond to our emotions, and when we're in the grip of strong feelings, it's hard to calibrate how we express them in conversation. The solution is to practice. By having more feedback conversations, we learn not only how specific individuals respond to us but also how we express our emotions in helpful and unhelpful ways.

Play Fair

You're sure to elicit a threat response if you provide feedback the other person views as unfair or inaccurate. But how do you avoid that, given how subjective perceptions of fairness and accuracy are?

David Bradford of the Stanford Graduate School of Business suggests "staying on our side of the net"—that is, focusing our feedback on our feelings about the behavior and avoiding references to the other person's motives. We're in safe territory on *our* side of the net; others may not like what we say when we describe how we feel, but they can't dispute its accuracy. However, when we make guesses about their motives, we cross over to *their* side of the net, and even minor inaccuracies can provoke a defensive reaction.

For example, when giving critical feedback to someone who's habitually late, it's tempting to say something like, "You don't value my time, and it's very disrespectful of you." But these are guesses about the other person's state of mind, not statements of fact. If we're even slightly off base, the employee will feel misunderstood and be less receptive to the feedback. A more effective way to make the same point is to say, "When you're late, I feel devalued and disrespected." It's a subtle distinction, but by focusing on the specific behavior and our internal response—by staying on our side of the net—we avoid making an inaccurate, disputable guess.

Because motives are often unclear, we constantly cross the net in an effort to make sense of others' behavior. While this is inevitable, it's good practice to notice when we're guessing someone's motives and get back on our side of the net before offering feedback.

Set the Stage

It's easy to take our surroundings for granted, but they have a big impact on any interaction. Paying attention to logistical details like these will help make your feedback conversations more productive:

- **Timing.** Although I encourage shorter, informal feedback conversations (see the end of this chapter), sometimes it's necessary to have a longer, in-depth discussion. When that's the case, be deliberate about scheduling. Instead of simply fitting it into an available slot on your calendar, choose a time when you and the other person will both be at your best, such as at the beginning of the day, before you're preoccupied with other issues, or at the end of the day, when you can spend more time in reflection. Think about the activities you and your employee will be engaged in just before and just after the conversation. If either of you are coming from (or heading to) a stressful experience, you'll be better off finding another time.

- **Duration.** We often put events on our calendars for a standard amount of time without considering what's needed for each interaction. Think about how much time a given feedback conversation is likely to take if it goes well—and if it goes poorly. You don't want to get into a meaningful discussion with an employee and suddenly find that you're late for your next meeting. Also, consider what you'll do if the conversation goes worse (or better) than expected. How bad (or good) will it have to be for you to ignore the next event on your calendar in order to continue the conversation?

- **Physical location.** Meeting in your office will reinforce hierarchical roles, which can be useful when you need to establish some distance between yourself and the other person—but this will also induce stress and increase the odds of a threat response. A less formal setting—such as a conference room, a restaurant, or even outdoors—will put you on a more even footing and reduce the likelihood of a threat response. Choose a location that suits the needs of the conversation, ensures sufficient privacy, and minimizes interruptions and distractions.

- **Proximity.** When meeting with an employee in an office or a conference room, sitting across from each other—with a desk or table in between—

creates physical distance, emphasizing your respective roles and reinforcing your authority. But you don't always want to do that. When you're trying to create a stronger connection with the other person or convey a greater sense of empathy, it's preferable to sit closer and on adjoining sides of the table or desk. Think about the optimal proximity between you and the other person at that moment. Perhaps even being seated is too formal, and you should go for a walk.

With a little practice, these guidelines will help you improve your feedback skills. As with any skill you're trying to master, experiment in low-risk situations before jumping into a high-stakes feedback conversation. Here are some ways to get started:

- **Have feedback conversations more often.** We associate feedback with performance reviews, but they're not good opportunities to improve our feedback skills because they're so infrequent and they tend to be stressful. Rather than saving up feedback for an employee on a wide range of topics, try offering smaller pieces of focused feedback on a regular basis. Even a two-minute debrief with an employee after a meeting or a presentation can be a useful learning opportunity for both of you.

- **Role-play difficult conversations.** With clients in my coaching practice and with my MBA students at Stanford, I've found that role-playing is a highly effective way to prepare to deliver challenging feedback. Conduct this exercise with a friendly colleague: Start by delivering your feedback while your colleague role-plays the recipient, which will allow you to try out different approaches. Then have your colleague give you the same feedback while you role-play the recipient. You'll learn from your colleague's approach, and you'll see the conversation from your employee's point of view. The preparation will help you refine your delivery and feel more relaxed in the actual conversation.

- **Ask for feedback yourself.** By asking employees to give you feedback on your effectiveness as a leader and manager, you'll benefit in three ways: You'll get valuable input, you'll understand what it's like to be on the receiving end, and your willingness to listen will make your own feedback mean more. If you sense that employees are reluctant to give you feedback, ask them to help you accomplish some specific goals, such as being more concise or interrupting less often. By acknowledging your own areas for improvement, you'll make it easier for them to speak up.

Ed Batista is an executive coach and an instructor at the Stanford Graduate School of Business. He writes regularly on issues related to coaching and professional development at www.edbatista.com, and he is currently writing a book on self-coaching for Harvard Business Review Press.

Chapter 7
Enlist Knowledge Coaches

A summary of the full-length HBR article "Deep Smarts," by **Dorothy Leonard** *and* **Walter Swap,** *highlighting key ideas.*

THE IDEA IN BRIEF

It takes years for your company's best people to acquire their expertise—but only seconds for them to walk out the door when opportunity beckons. And when they go, they take their deep smarts with them. Deeply smart people make intuitive decisions fast and spot problems and possibilities others miss. Informed by almost preternaturally sound judgment and a gut sense for

Adapted from *Harvard Business Review,* September 2004 (product #7731)

interrelationships, they see the big picture—rather than getting bogged down in details. Their wisdom is crucial to your company's survival.

How to capture the deep smarts residing in your organization? Turn your experts into knowledge coaches. Knowledge coaches use learn-by-doing techniques— guided practice, observation, problem solving, and experimentation—to help novices absorb long-acquired business wisdom.

Knowledge coaching not only spurs transfer and retention of vital wisdom, it yields breakthrough product ideas and more efficient business processes. Can your company afford *not* to invest in it?

THE IDEA IN PRACTICE

Consider these knowledge coaching techniques:

Guided practice

Novices practice skills under the watchful eye of knowledge coaches, who then provide feedback that allows them to refine their new capabilities.

> *Example:* At SAIC, new consultants learn their trade from seasoned colleagues through a "see one, lead one, teach one" process. First, they observe an expert helping a client solve a specific problem. Next, they practice their skills by leading a client session, receiving feedback from the knowledge coach. Then, they teach those skills to another consultant.

Guided observation

This technique takes two forms—shadowing and field trips. Through *shadowing*, novices absorb deep smarts by following experienced, skilled colleagues, and then discussing their observations with those colleagues. One junior consultant who sat in on client meetings and then analyzed his observations with an older colleague contended, "I learned more from those debriefs than in four years at my prior company and two years of business school."

During *field trips*, novices break out of rigid mental habits and expand their experience through exposure to novel ways of thinking and behaving.

Example: On field trips to Mexico, Korea, and a U.S. specialty toy store, teams from retailer Best Buy observed young people engaged in communal play focused on a product (such as a doll) or technology (such as video games). These visits spurred ideas for providing socially oriented experiences in Best Buy stores. For instance, the company's engineers developed "PCBang," which enables teens and people in their early twenties—much younger than Best Buy's typical customer—to play computer games and socialize.

Guided problem solving

Knowledge coaches and protégés work on problems jointly, so protégés learn how to approach problems.

Example: A senior engineer renowned for his ability to bring multiple perspectives to the design of complex products had his protégé spend several months on the assembly line tackling problems with a test technician. The senior engineer joined many of these sessions, adding perspectives the technician lacked—such as customer preferences. The protégé acquired comprehensive know-how about the product, from design to production to fulfillment of customers' needs.

Guided experimentation

Knowledge coaches help novices set up modest experiments that speed learning.

Example: Start-up company ActivePhoto had developed a technology for instantly downloading and cataloging digital photographs. To determine its most profitable market, the firm conducted pilot studies with three promising customer bases: public emergency services, insurance-claims processing, and online auctioning. Through discussions of each experiment's results with knowledge coaches, Active-Photo quickly eliminated the first market.

Dorothy Leonard is the William J. Abernathy Professor Emerita of Business Administration at Harvard Business School in Boston. **Walter Swap** is a professor emeritus of psychology at Tufts University in Medford, Massachusetts. They are the coauthors of *Deep Smarts: How to Cultivate and Transfer Enduring Business Wisdom* (Harvard Business School Publishing, 2005) and *Critical Knowledge Transfer: Tools for Managing Your Company's Deep Smarts* (Harvard Business Review Press, December 2014).

Chapter 8
Coaching Effectively in Less Time

by Daisy Wademan Dowling

Virtually all of the young executives I work with want to be good managers and mentors. They just don't have the time—or so they believe. "I could either bring in a new deal, or I could take one of my people out for lunch to talk about their career," a financial services leader told me recently. "In this industry and in this market, which one do you think I'm going to pick?"

Good question. It's not easy to help your employees develop even as you take advantage of every business opportunity, but you can make coaching easier on yourself in three ways: planning coaching time well, giving

Adapted from content posted on hbr.org on February 3, 2009

feedback efficiently, and making use of found time to coach when you can.

Plan Coaching Time Well

Set aside time to think about and pursue issues with your team. Keep each of these sessions brief, but make them regular: Put a 30-minute weekly recurring item on your calendar, for example, and don't let yourself slip into re-scheduling or working through it.

Use this window to think about your team's actions over the past week. Who needs praise? Motivation? Better prioritization skills? Feedback on a lousy presentation? To be told to wear a tie to the office? You may notice these things in passing, but if you don't schedule time to focus on them, you'll find yourself worrying about them all week—on the way to the office, in meetings about other things—and never actually address them.

Also use this time to check in on your direct reports' progress and development more broadly. Do you have a new employee whose needs and interests you want to get to know better? A mentee who has asked for help developing a particular skill? A direct report you haven't really touched base with recently? Instead of having to find the time to plan their coaching, you can use the window you've already set aside.

Once you've identified the issues that need addressing, use the remainder of the time to drop a congratulatory e-mail, to walk over to your direct report and give her some quick feedback (more on this later), or, if the situation warrants, to set up time to hold a formal coaching session.

Your strategy here is containment: Scheduling windows to think about and address coaching issues lets you limit them to a manageable amount of time.

Give Feedback Efficiently

Once you've identified that you need to give feedback to a direct report, you can make that process more efficient in three ways.

- **Create a standard way in.** For the majority of managers, providing feedback—particularly constructive feedback—is stressful and requires significant forethought. How should you bring up the bungled analysis, the hurdles to promotion, or even the meeting that went unusually well? Like chess masters, we spend most of our time contemplating the first move. That's why the key to reducing the time you spend mulling over and preparing for each coaching conversation is to have a standard way in: a simple, routinized way to open discussions about performance. Keep it simple, and announce directly what's to come. A straightforward "I'm going to give you some feedback" or "Are you open to my coaching on this?" gets immediate attention and sets the right tone. It will make it easier to prepare for the game if you have your opener ready. Furthermore, your direct reports will become familiar with your opener, and that will help them be attuned to and hear the feedback more clearly.

- **Be blunt.** The number one mistake executives make in coaching and delivering feedback to their people is being insufficiently candid—typically, because they don't want to be mean. If you've ever used the phrase "maybe you could . . ." in a coaching conversation or asked one of your people to "think about" a performance issue, there's a 99% probability you're not being blunt enough. But the more candid you are, the more likely your coachee is to hear your message, and thus the more likely you are to have impact, and quickly. The trick to being candid without feeling like an ogre? Be honest, be sincere, be personal—while addressing the issue head-on. The best feedback I ever received came a few years into my career, directly after a terrible meeting I had with senior management, in which I had been both unprepared and defensive. As we rode down in the elevator afterward, my boss said quietly, "Next time, I expect you to do better." Don't dance around the issues, and don't let the person you're coaching do so either.

- **Ask him to play it back.** If your feedback doesn't end up sticking, you'll need to deliver it a second time—and a third, and a fourth—all of which takes your valuable time and managerial energy. To avoid the need for encore performances, check to make sure you've made an impact on the first go-round by asking the person you're coaching to paraphrase what he heard. If your coachee can clearly explain to you—in his own words—what he needs to change or do next, that goes a long way to ensuring he's gotten the message. You'll then know that the conversation is over and you can get back to other things. If the message is muddled, you can correct it immediately. In either case, you've limited the need for future follow-up.

Use Found Time

If you plan and use your coaching time wisely, you'll find that you can maintain your coaching relationships and get your other work done as well. But what if you're in a crunch period or for some other reason just can't find the minutes to spare for your weekly check-in? If that's the case, use what I call the 3.1% coaching method: Limit your people-development activities to no more than 15 incremental minutes per day. That's 75 minutes a week, or 3.1% of a hypothetical 40-hour workweek. Here's how to find those 15 minutes.

- **Turn dead time into development time.** Walking back to your office after a meeting? Use those two minutes to give your direct report feedback on the presentation and on how he could do better next time. He didn't have a speaking role? Ask how he thought the meeting went and how he might have made certain points differently—and then offer feedback on that. Direct, in-the-moment feedback is your single best tool for developing people. Look for every two-minute stretch in your day during which you could be talking to someone else—most often, that's travel time—and convert those windows into coaching opportunities.

Walking down to the corner to get a cup of coffee? Ask one of your employees to come along—and talk about goals and priorities. Driving to the airport? Check in with an employee or two over the phone.

- **Make two calls per day.** On your way home from work, call (or e-mail) two people you met with that day and offer "feedforward": "I like what you've done with the Smithers account. Next time, let's try to keep marketing costs down. Thanks for your hard work." Always make "thank you" a part of the message. Employees who feel appreciated, and know that you're trying to develop their skills, stay engaged over the long run.

- **Show up in her work space.** Once per day, get up and walk over to the desk of one of your direct reports. Take two minutes to ask her what she's working on. Once she's finished answering, respond, "What do you need from me to make that project/transaction successful?" The goal is for her to hear you saying, "I know who you are, I've got high expectations—and I've got your back."

With consistent (read: daily) use, these strategies will pay off. Your employees will feel that you're not just their boss, but a coach. They'll sharpen their skills *and* stay motivated.

And for any manager, that's time well spent.

Daisy Wademan Dowling serves as managing director and head of talent development for the Blackstone Group, the global asset management firm. She is also the author of *Remember Who You Are* (Harvard Business Review Press, 2004) and a regular contributor to HBR.

Chapter 9
Help People Help Themselves

by Ed Batista

When I take on new clients in my executive coaching practice, I emphasize how much work they will be doing *without* me. That's because they typically spend just 1% of their working hours in coaching sessions; the other 99% of the time, they're managing interactions, making choices, and solving problems on their own. Although our conversations may influence my clients as they go about their day-to-day activities, most of the time they're *coaching themselves*. They're assessing what's working and what's not, deciding where to change course and where to hold steady, and repeating this process as they steer themselves through professional challenges.

The same holds true for your employees if you manage knowledge workers who operate with little, if any, direct supervision. You check in with them regularly to plan, prioritize, and assess progress toward goals, but you don't peer over their shoulders all day, telling them how to complete each task. You don't have time to provide such detailed guidance—and even if you did, they would perceive it as intrusive micromanagement.

This constraint actually presents a tremendous opportunity: You can be a more effective leader and manager by helping your employees coach themselves. To be clear, "self-coaching" is not a solitary process but, rather, a self-directed one. Your employees will continue to need your guidance and support, but their "coaching" shouldn't just be a series of formal discussions with you. It's a tool they can use on their own or in any conversation with anyone.

Here's how you can get them started.

Foster a Growth Mind-Set

As discussed earlier in this guide, people have two basic mind-sets about development: Those with a *fixed mind-set* view qualities such as intelligence and talent as predetermined and unchanging, while those with a *growth mind-set* believe that these qualities can be enhanced through dedication and effort. (See chapter 1, "Shift Your Thinking to Coach Effectively.") Research by Stanford psychologist Carol Dweck demonstrates not only the impact of mind-set on performance but also the relative ease with which people can shift mind-sets. As she has observed, "Just by knowing about the two mind-sets, you can start thinking and reacting in new ways."

A growth mind-set yields substantial benefits in a self-coaching context: When people view themselves as works in progress, they remain open to learning and change. They're more persistent in seeking solutions to problems, more resilient in the face of setbacks, and more receptive to critical feedback. They also learn more from their mistakes, as research by Michigan State psychologist Jason Moser indicates, in part because they don't get as upset by failures, and they spend more time assessing what went wrong.

Encouraging a growth mind-set doesn't mean simply offering praise and avoiding criticism; it means focusing your feedback—both positive and negative—on employees' efforts to accomplish their goals, not on their inherent abilities. When we praise people for their talents or criticize them for their inadequacies, they adopt a fixed mind-set, undermining their attempts to self-coach. But when we praise them for their determination and criticize flagging effort, they're more likely to adopt a growth mind-set, which makes self-coaching easier and more fruitful.

You can further support a growth mind-set by viewing setbacks as learning opportunities. While you should

---

SELF-COACHING TIP

High achievers are as likely as underperformers to have a fixed mind-set. Promote a growth mind-set by emphasizing the value of determination and persistence—not just strengths and achievements—when reviewing their performance. Encourage them to do the same in their self-assessments.

provide candid feedback when employees fail, emphasize the value of learning from the experience. Respond to failures with an attitude of curiosity and a commitment to understanding root causes, and highlight areas where greater determination or persistence might have resulted in success.

Ask Before You Advise

As longtime MIT management professor Edgar Schein cautions in *Helping,* dispensing wisdom prematurely is a trap for anyone seeking to help others, and it's particularly dangerous for a manager guiding a direct report. When an employee presents you with a problem, you probably feel an immediate urge to respond with a solution. That may seem like a logical and efficient way to provide support, but it comes at a price. You limit the range of possible solutions to your own ideas, diminish your employees' ownership of the situation, and increase their dependence on you. (Again, see chapter 1, "Shift Your Thinking to Coach Effectively.")

Resisting that urge is a critical step in helping your employees coach themselves. By backing off just a bit, you'll compel them to fully tap their own knowledge and expertise—which may be more extensive than yours— and encourage them to take greater responsibility and act more independently. So when an employee seeks your support, start by asking questions, not giving answers. Follow these guidelines:

- **Avoid questions that invite "Yes" or "No" answers.** These questions are direct, but that's not always an

Help People Help Themselves

advantage. The downside in a self-coaching context is that they stop the conversation just when you want the other person to reflect more deeply on his or her experience.

- **Embrace questions that sound naive.** Although sophisticated questions may demonstrate your understanding of a situation's complexities, they also put the emphasis on your own expertise. Simple, open-ended questions such as "What will success look like?" and "What challenges will you face?" are more useful in challenging the other person to think creatively.

- **Use "Why . . ." questions with care.** Asking people why they did something can help them step back and reassess their approach, but it can also trigger defensive rationalization. That's less likely to

SELF-COACHING TIP

Emphasize your role as a questioner rather than a source of solutions, and encourage employees to engage others in the same way. They can turn any conversation into a self-coaching dialogue simply by asking their peers and colleagues to pose questions before offering advice. Note the questions that draw out the most meaningful answers, and suggest that your employees ask similar questions of themselves when facing a challenge or looking back on an experience.

happen with "How . . ." and "What . . ." questions such as "How do you feel about what happened?" and "What would you do differently?"—which don't sound accusatory.

Of course, your employees sometimes need your advice—but wait for those moments and jump in as necessary, not as a first response to every problem they face. To reassure those who simply want to be given an answer, you might say, "I'll be happy to offer my opinion later, but, first, what do you think?"

Be Transparent

While your employees may pick up tips on self-coaching by observing how you coach them, you'll make it easier for them to replicate the process—both on their own and in coaching conversations with others—by talking openly about the techniques you're using. This transparency will also help them understand why you're behaving differ-

SELF-COACHING TIP

Leave a few minutes at the end of every coaching session to discuss the conversation itself. Talk about why it was helpful—and what might have made it even more helpful. Spell out which coaching techniques you used and ask for feedback. Encourage your employees to use the methods that worked best when they initiate coaching conversations with others.

ently if new coaching techniques involve a change in your management style.

For example, if your employees are accustomed to coming to you for answers—and you've readily supplied them—a sudden emphasis on asking questions may feel jarring or frustrating to them unless you provide context for it. Explain why you're asking the questions and what benefits you hope to obtain by doing so.

When your employees see what coaching techniques you're using, they can share with you what works best for them (not all techniques work equally well for everyone). And that understanding will feed their self-coaching efforts. They'll benefit more from individual reflection when they step back from their coaching with you and articulate its impact on their actions.

Then, by asking colleagues and friends to adopt the same techniques they've found effective in conversations with you, they can recruit new, supportive members of their self-coaching team. You'll continue to be a key member of that team, of course, but you won't need to be there for every coaching conversation or experience.

———————————

Ed Batista is an executive coach and an instructor at the Stanford Graduate School of Business. He writes regularly on issues related to coaching and professional development at www.edbatista.com, and he is currently writing a book on self-coaching for Harvard Business Review Press.

Chapter 10
Avoid Common Coaching Mistakes

by Muriel Maignan Wilkins

Managers learning to coach are often eager to use their newly honed skills with their staff. But even a few missteps can easily discourage managers from committing to coaching their employees over the long haul. Here are four common mistakes made by managers learning to coach, as well as guidance on how to avoid—and correct—them.

Common Mistake 1: Coaching the "Mini-Me"

Coaching is about helping your team member reach her own potential. Yet, time and time again, managers instead try to coach individuals into the managers' own image. Don't fall into the trap of trying to coach your team member into a replica of yourself, or she will become rapidly disengaged from the coaching process. Both your attempt to support her and her attempt to deliver will prove unsustainable in the long term.

One of my clients made this mistake early on. As a manager learning to coach, he enthusiastically provided his staff members with advice and individualized guidance for their professional development. But rather than letting them develop their own paths and learn from their own successes and mistakes, he typically began his coaching conversations with "Well, if it were me . . ." His coaching didn't stick, and he, as well as his direct reports, got frustrated with the efforts.

Remedy

Coaching is not about you—and it's certainly not about creating another you. Your team member has different strengths and weaknesses from you, and different interests and goals. To ensure that your coaching is centered on the employee and not on you, you have to meet him where he is in terms of skill, capability, and commitment to the assignment at hand. Before you craft advice to share with him, start by understanding his strengths and weaknesses and identify how they differ from yours. Take his understanding of the situation into account by asking questions. Consider how he looks at the situation. Then you can frame your suggestions and feedback based on realistic expectations.

Common Mistake 2: Thinking Coaching Is Special Time

Managers often overly mystify coaching and as a result make the perennial mistake of waiting for the right time to coach. And, unfortunately, that right time often never comes, because making coaching larger than life makes it unattainable and impractical even for the best of us. And so all our best-laid coaching plans never come to fruition.

Remedy

You do not need to wait for a special time to coach, and not every coaching conversation needs to be a big development discussion with a capital *D*. The best coaching is integrated into your and the employee's day-to-day work life. Make it a practice to coach in the moment. If your employee is about to prepare for something, proactively spend a few minutes coaching him on how he will approach the deliverable. If he has completed an assignment, debrief with some coaching questions that will help him learn from the experience and use the knowledge for the next time around.

Certainly you should still hold scheduled sit-down discussions with your direct reports to discuss their development goals and a plan of action, but don't wait for those meetings. If you do, you'll miss the opportunity to give feedback in real time, and you'll also put such weight on those bigger meetings that they will be emotionally fraught and less productive.

Common Mistake 3: Losing Your Patience

Coaching requires patience. It is not about pushing or pulling your team members directly to the specific results you want them to achieve; it's more like watching on the sidelines during game time, letting them find their own way.

For example, over her years as an analyst, Paula had carefully developed a very distinct way of analyzing her division's end-of-month reports. Now the division manager, she has become increasingly frustrated with the way the new analyst approaches the reports; it seems inefficient and imprecise. Rather than invest the time to walk the analyst through her approach, however, Paula simply takes over and does it herself, figuring that it will take less time to do it correctly. Little does Paula recognize that in the long run she is doing a disservice to the analyst, to herself, and even to the organization by not teaching her hard-earned skills to her next-level staff.

For the results- and action-oriented drivers among us, however, stepping back and letting your direct report make mistakes—or just different choices from those you would have made—can feel like a tortuous process. Especially when you're short on time, or when a project is particularly important, it is easy to lose your patience: You may look flustered, let frustration creep into your voice, or simply snatch the task away and do it yourself. But giving in to your impatience in this way counteracts all your previous efforts by making your employee want to throw up his hands (if you've given up on him, why shouldn't he?).

Remedy

Resist the urge to succumb to the tiny voice inside telling you, "Oh, it would just be easier to tell him exactly what to do, or better yet, just do it myself already!" To approach coaching with composure, follow these guidelines.

- **Embrace the idea that coaching is not a quick-fix proposition.** Coaching is a marathon, not a sprint. Don't expect your direct report to move the needle from 0 to 10 after one opportunity to practice the skill when he's been without it for years. You should expect him to stumble a few times before he gets it. Just reminding yourself that you shouldn't expect to see results right away can put you in a better frame of mind. It also allows you to see when to celebrate a direct report's successes—even if his work isn't perfect.

- **Set a time line.** Even if you know it will take some time before your direct report has mastered this new skill, it can help you to cite a specific target date by which point you expect her to be independent. It can be motivating to her to have a target date, and helpful to you to estimate when you can depend on her to perform the task proficiently.

- **Establish clear milestones.** Don't wait until that target date to check in with your direct report to see how she is doing on the task. Instead, do so over the duration of the project by breaking down the assignment into smaller chunks. This will enable you to coach her along the way rather than in retrospect; it will also satiate your need to see progress and movement on the assignment. Your direct report will also gain confidence as she accomplishes each milestone or corrects the course successfully.

- **Watch your tone.** In the moment, as with all professional communication, take a deep breath if you feel yourself getting flustered or about to make a snap decision because something just seems so easy for you and apparently hard for your direct report. And if you do slip into backseat-driver mode, be courageous enough to apologize.

Common Mistake 4: Assuming Everyone Is Coachable

Patience is important in coaching, but sometimes managers can be too patient.

John was frustrated and discouraged with one of his employees. He'd spent an inordinate amount of time coaching her on meeting deadlines on time, to no avail. She simply made no efforts to try doing anything differently. John kept trying new ways to engage her, but he wasn't getting anywhere.

No matter how much of an optimist you are, sometimes you need to be realistic: Like John, you may have an employee who is not coachable—or not coachable at this time. Many managers fail to recognize this situation, and subsequently they exert far more energy than needed, with little results.

Remedy

A person must want to be coached in order for it to work, because ultimately the responsibility and ownership of the effort are hers. Start by giving your team member the benefit of the doubt, but as you work with her, quickly assess her coachability. From what you've seen, does she want to learn? Is she trying (even if she's not succeeding)? Does she seem genuinely appreciative of the coaching?

If you're not sure, talk to her about it. Give some feedback on how you've seen her approach the coaching you've given; how she responds to such a conversation can be very telling about how much this is something she actually wants.

In the rare cases in which you discover that you really are dealing with someone who is not coachable, don't hesitate to try a strategy other than coaching rather than waste your energy. In certain situations, it may be appropriate to take a more directive stance. And in situations where performance is severely affected despite many attempts at coaching, you should consider whether your direct report is in the right role.

Learning to be an effective coach as a manager takes lots of practice. Over time, you will hone your skill and build your repertoire of tried-and-true strategies that help you effectively develop your employees. Although these remedies are meant to help you get there more efficiently, don't be concerned if you trip up every now and then on any of these pitfalls or others you might encounter. As with the staff members you are coaching, some of your best learning will often come through your mistakes.

––––––––––

Muriel Maignan Wilkins is the cofounder and managing partner of Paravis Partners, a Washington, D.C.–based leadership coaching and consulting firm. Previously, she held various advisory and leadership roles in marketing and strategy at Prudential, Accenture, and *U.S. News & World Report.* She is the coauthor with Amy Jen Su of *Own the Room: Discover Your Signature Voice to Master Your Leadership Presence* (Harvard Business Review Press, 2013).

Section 3
Customize Your Coaching

Chapter 11
Tailor Your Coaching to People's Learning Styles

by David A. Kolb and Kay Peterson

As you coach your employees to develop their skills or improve their performance, you can set them up for success by understanding how they learn best and adjusting your methods accordingly. They may prefer learning through intense experience, sustained reflection, analytical thinking, goal-directed action, or a combination of approaches (the basic steps in what we call the Experiential Learning Cycle—see figure 11-1). By tapping into their preferred styles, you will engage them more deeply and motivate them. As a result, they'll make greater—and faster—progress toward their goals.

FIGURE 11-1

The Experiential Learning Cycle

The people you coach learn through experience: They think about it, extrapolate lessons from it, and experiment with those lessons—which leads to new experiences and learning.

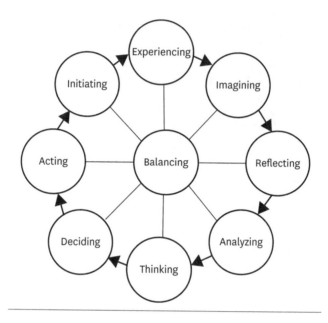

If the benefits of customized coaching are so clear, why don't more managers do it? Largely because we tend to favor our own learning preferences when we teach others (see table 11-1). We assume that what works for us will work for everyone else, but that's just not the case.

Take Marie, a vice president of operations for a national manufacturing company. She had a quick, decisive learning style—and struggled to coach direct reports whose styles differed from hers. Rather than let them

TABLE 11-1

Questions to help you coach more holistically

When coaching people whose learning styles don't match yours, you must communicate in a way that resonates with *them*. Try asking yourself the following questions as prompts for the different styles. They'll help you customize your coaching to your employees—whether they favor Reflecting, Initiating, or another approach entirely—instead of retreating to your own comfort zone.

INITIATING	EXPERIENCING	IMAGINING
How can I inspire my employee to learn?	Am I fully present (without distractions) during each coaching session?	Am I listening and receptive?
What questions can I ask to promote discovery?	Am I attending to the relationship?	Should we explore more diverse sources of information?
What experiments will help my employee apply the lessons learned?	Am I connecting emotionally?	Am I helping my employee explore all possibilities?
Can I provide opportunities to influence others?	Am I making my employee feel supported?	Have I judged too soon?
Am I bringing enough energy to our coaching sessions?		Have I shown empathy?

REFLECTING	ANALYZING	THINKING
Have I asked thought-provoking questions?	Have I articulated a thorough, precise coaching plan?	What is the larger plan for development or improvement?
Am I allowing time for my employee to "struggle" and find answers?	Can I use a model or theory to explain it?	Have I been objective and logical, setting aside my emotions and self-interest?
Can I slow things down?	Can I provide data or specialized knowledge to support it?	Am I stepping back to generalize and articulate lessons learned?
Have I considered other points of view?	Are my thoughts organized?	How can I structure our sessions differently?
Have I observed and deliberated?	Am I presenting ideas logically?	Am I assessing costs and benefits?

(continued)

TABLE 11-1 (CONTINUED)

DECIDING	ACTING	BALANCING
What is the goal of the session?	What can we get done now?	What are my employee's blind spots?
How will I know if we have reached it?	Are we considering both the task and the people it will affect?	Which skills does this situation call for—and which ones are missing?
What practical results can we achieve?	Am I encouraging my employee to take risks?	Are we considering all options when setting development goals and deciding how to meet them?
Is it time to choose a course of action?	What activities will support my employee's learning and help him or her apply it?	
Can I provide direct, immediate feedback?		

take the lead, she jumped in to help them solve each challenge as soon as they encountered it. Things got done her way, but people weren't really learning—and she became frustrated with their lack of growth.

But then she recognized how she'd contributed to the problem: She hadn't allowed people to take enough responsibility for their own development, nor had she considered their approaches to learning. She turned the situation around by taking the time to identify her employees' learning styles and changing her coaching tactics to suit them.

When coaching Tyler, for example, Marie discovered through observation and conversations with him that his preferred style was Experiencing, or learning through feelings and relationships. (See the following section "What Are Your Employees' Learning Styles?" for more on recognizing preferences.) So she resisted the urge to set goals and take action right away, as she usually did.

Instead, she connected with him emotionally first, asking how he felt about his team's relationships and revealing her own feelings about working on a team, which conveyed her support and established trust.

One of Tyler's goals was to overcome his fear of difficult conversations and handle them better. Together, he and Marie identified a way of conquering that fear: organizing his thoughts before trying to communicate them. Tyler then practiced by role-playing with Marie. (He felt comfortable doing so because of the personal connection they had established.) Because the learning process reflected his style, he became more invested in it—and his skills improved each time he practiced.

What Are Your Employees' Learning Styles?

Personality type, education, and cultural background all influence learning preferences. And once someone finds success with a certain style, she'll continue to rely on it, reinforcing the preference.

Here are the nine learning styles you may recognize in members of your team and the coaching tactics that complement them:

1. **Initiating: experimenting with new courses of action.** These learners enjoy networking, influencing others, thinking on their feet, and seeking opportunities. Encourage them to jump in and learn from trial and error. Use inspiring, energetic language to communicate with them (*set the pace, grab the chance, seize the opportunity*).

2. **Experiencing: finding meaning from deep involvement in experiences and relationships.** These learners focus on emotions and intuition. Connect with them on a personal level and encourage them to work with others. Use language that is sensitive and accepting (*touched, grounded, present, mindful*).

3. **Imagining: contemplating experiences and considering a range of solutions.** These learners seek and appreciate diverse input from many people. Listen to their many creative ideas before prompting them to focus on one. Encourage them to discover a course of action through a series of small decisions. Use words that convey open-mindedness, empathy, and trust (*value ideas, brainstorm, reach for the stars, create an ideal vision, consider other perspectives*).

4. **Reflecting: connecting experiences and ideas through sustained reflection.** These learners observe others, take multiple perspectives into account, and wait to act until they're confident about the outcome. Allow adequate time for them to watch, listen, and rehearse quietly on their own. Communicate with words that convey a slow and thoughtful approach (*take plenty of time, be cautious, pause, process the idea, watch a role model*).

5. **Analyzing: integrating and systematizing ideas.** These learners like to make plans, attend to de-

tails, and use theories to test assumptions. Provide conceptual models so they can process ideas before applying them. Use concise, logical language (*seek details, organize the facts, synthesize the data, do the research, make a plan*).

6. **Thinking: engaging in disciplined logic or mathematics.** These learners prefer quantitative analysis and abstract reasoning, and tend to focus on one objective at a time. Engage them by weighing costs and benefits. Communicate using the language of logic and reason (*see the point, just the facts, sharpen our focus, create a spreadsheet, examine the data*).

7. **Deciding: choosing a single course of action early on to achieve practical results.** These learners efficiently set goals and critically evaluate whatever solution they've chosen. Involve them in figuring out which problems to solve and setting standards, and allow them to measure their own success. Use language that's pragmatic and direct (*take a practical approach, measure success, critical feedback, strong direction, best practice*).

8. **Acting: taking assertive, goal-directed steps toward change.** These learners care about completing tasks *and* meeting people's needs, and they take risks to get things done faster and better. Encourage trial and error and on-the-job experiments. Choose words that

convey dynamism and speed (*take action, quick turnaround, achieve results, implement the plan*).

9. **Balancing: weighing the pros and cons of acting versus reflecting, and experiencing versus thinking.** These learners can flexibly assume any learning style to fill gaps in their knowledge. Tap their abilities to identify blind spots and to adapt. Communicate with language that reflects their flexibility (*balance the situation, include variety, adapt, take a holistic perspective*).

Do any of your direct reports, like Tyler, learn best through feelings and relationships (Experiencing or Imagining)? Which ones prefer watching role models from a safe distance and emulating their behavior (Reflecting)? Which are comfortable with trial and error (Initiating or Acting)? To find out, try asking employees whether they *generally* gravitate toward feeling, watching, thinking, or acting—and map their answers to the learning styles defined above.

But that's just a start. (You'll probably get uneven responses—many people haven't even thought about their learning preferences and may struggle to articulate them.) So add your own observations to the mix: What appears to interest and motivate each employee? Knowing that can shed light on learning preferences. For example, an employee who always emerges from your group's annual strategy off-site with renewed enthusiasm, rallying others to support the mission and business model, is likely to have an Initiating style. By contrast, someone who avoids deliberating but digs into every task with energy and commitment probably has an Acting style of learning.

Language cues can also be telling: Note whether employees favor expressions of feeling, believing, thinking, or doing. Someone who often talks in emotional-relational terms ("I loved the discussion we had" or "The financials are making me anxious") probably focuses on feelings and learns by Experiencing rather than Thinking or Deciding.

What If Their Styles Aren't Doing the Trick?

Knowing how people like to learn will accelerate their overall development—but using only their preferred styles won't help them tackle every challenge they face. They'll often need to try out new styles to meet their goals.

Consider Alex, an accountant who has been promoted to lead his department. His primary learning style is Analyzing; he also relies on Thinking and Deciding, though to a lesser extent. This approach has served him well as an individual contributor. But to thrive in his new leadership position, he'll need to expand his repertoire of backup styles to include Initiating, Experiencing, and Imagining.

Now suppose you are his manager. You can help him experiment with these learning styles and strengthen his use of them through practice. Ask him to facilitate a brainstorming session, for instance, to become better at Imagining as he envisions new possibilities for the group. Develop his capacity for Initiating by assigning him to a cross-functional project, where his success will depend in part on his ability to influence people who don't report to him. Work with him to build key relationships so he'll spend more time Experiencing—introduce him to colleagues whose styles differ from (and complement) his. During your regular check-ins, talk about these experiments in order to make the learning explicit and deliberate. Ask him what he's enjoying and what he finds challenging. See what lessons he can tease out on his own; if he struggles to do that, refer him back to the Learning Cycle—remind him which styles will help him succeed as a department head.

As he's trying out new styles, however, you will still want to use data, frameworks, theories, and goal setting to motivate him, given his natural preference for Analyzing, Thinking, and Deciding. To get him to sharpen his networking skills, for instance, make the interpersonal challenge more appealing to him by enhancing it with analysis: Ask him to map out his current network and identify which people's functions and expertise will help him most in his new role.

To do everything we're suggesting, you'll need to *really* know your employees—talk to them, observe them, analyze them, ask colleagues about them. Since individuals' learning preferences are so deeply ingrained, your coaching will be more efficient and fruitful if you meet people where they are in the Learning Cycle. Yet it's equally important to recognize when their styles aren't panning out. By playing to their preferences—while also encouraging them to become more flexible—you'll help them discover and reach their potential.

David A. Kolb, a psychologist and educational theorist, is the founder of Experience Based Learning Systems and a professor emeritus at Case Western Reserve University. His renowned Kolb Learning Style Inventory is outlined briefly in this chapter. **Kay Peterson,** a principal at Learning Partners Group, is an organizational development consultant and coach specializing in experiential learning and learning-style flexibility.

Chapter 12
Coaching Your Stars, Steadies, and Strugglers

by Jim Grinnell

Let's say you have three direct reports: Cindy always exceeds her numbers, rarely asks for your help, and often takes initiative on new projects. Performancewise, she's every manager's dream, although she can be abrasive and dismissive of her colleagues. Compare her with Ed, a pleasant colleague who gets the job done competently. His attitude is "a day's work for a day's pay," and for him that day ends at 5:00 PM. And then there's Sam. He's very likeable, but he can't seem to get things right. It's heartbreaking—he stays late every day and

---

Adapted from "The ABCs of Employee Coaching," posted on May 31, 2012, at businesslearningcoach.com

takes work home on the weekends just to perform at a subpar level.

How do you coach Cindy, Ed, and Sam? Should you give them equal time? Should you emphasize the same things?

This may sound unfair, but you cannot treat them the same way. You need to make some choices—place some bets on where your efforts will pay off.

The Stars

We often assume it's best to leave A players like Cindy alone. They've mastered their domain, and we don't want to muck things up, so we keep our distance as managers.

But that's a mistake. You should actually devote more coaching time to your stars than to anyone else because that's where you'll yield the greatest results. Plus, they need more support than you might think. As executive coach Steven Berglas points out in "How to Keep A Players Productive" (HBR September 2006), stars, "despite their veneer of self-satisfaction, smugness, and even bluster," are often insecure individuals in need of praise and nurturing. Many high performers grew up in an environment where great was never good enough. As a result, they often feel they're *masquerading* as successful.

When you coach A players, offset their insecurities with affirmation. Try the following suggestions, drawn from Berglas's article:

- **Praise your stars genuinely and frequently.** They'll immediately sniff out platitudes and empty accolades. When you praise them, focus on the skills and strengths they value in themselves. For instance, if a direct report says she gets charged up by landing high-margin sales deals, congratulate her when she does so. And if she responds well to public recognition, share the news in a department meeting or send out a group e-mail when she brings in a big account.

- **Rein them in.** Left to their own devices, A players will keep raising their own standards and over time will push themselves to performance they can't sustain. So act like a governor on an engine: Keep their expectations from revving to the point of breakdown. One way to do this is to discuss your concerns about their frenetic pace with them. They're self-focused, so they'll probably be receptive if you direct the conversation to *their* well-being.

- **Nudge them to play nicely.** A players tend to be hyper-judgmental of their colleagues. Unless you explicitly hold them accountable for collegiality and teamwork, they may create interpersonal turmoil, undermining their positive contributions. Sometimes they'll demonstrate annoyance when their teammates don't perform to their standards, or they'll act with contempt when asked to assist coworkers. When delivering constructive feedback to A players, comment on the behavior, not on the person (a lot of "you" statements may get their defenses up). And be specific about the impact of their behavior on the team's performance. That's something they'll care about.

High performers can be hard to take. It's tempting to bring them down a peg or two when they start acting up, but keep that impulse in check. You'll get much more out of them—and less grief—if you allow them to savor their accomplishments.

The Steadies

If A players are your lead singers and guitarists, B players such as Ed in the example earlier are your drummers and bass players. They certainly don't get top billing, but they hold everything together in the organization. B players make up the lion's share of the workforce—75% to 80%, by some estimates. And they dutifully get the job done with little fanfare or oversight.

Still, they need your attention. Here are some tips on coaching them effectively, based on insights from "Let's Hear It for B Players" (HBR June 2003), by Thomas J. DeLong and Vineeta Vijayaraghavan:

- **Accept them for who they are.** Some managers assume you should try to move your B players up to the A level. While this approach is intuitively appealing, it's not the best investment of your time, for a variety of reasons: Many B players have reached the limits of their abilities. Some have made a conscious life choice to occupy the meaty part of the performance curve because they're winding down their careers, for example, or seeking work/life balance. While a subset have A-level potential, the majority are entrenched at the B level. But these folks still bring tremendous value. They're often straight shooters who provide insights others are afraid to share. They are also less apt to leave—and thus disrupt—the organization.

- **Recognize and reward them.** Though they don't receive (or expect) the same financial rewards or promotions as A players, B players crave affirmation. If a B player puts in extra effort to respond to a customer complaint, acknowledge it. And deliver your praise however your employee likes to receive it. Some people prefer it one-on-one, while others seek public accolades.

- **Give them options.** B performers may not want to grow and develop as much as their A peers—but they don't want to stagnate, either. Provide opportunities for them to grow within their comfort zones. Invest in training that will help them shore up their strengths. Send them to conferences and seminars on topics they care about. Ask them to mentor junior employees. Solicit their input on decisions. B players have a lot to offer—but you need to make it relatively easy for them.

The Strugglers

Managers often devote most of their coaching to the employees who struggle the most, like Sam—and that's a losing proposition.

When we talk about C players, we're not referring to employees who are adjusting to the organization or to new roles; we're talking about individuals who *should be* performing at a higher level. Over time, they just don't carry their weight. They drag down their teams and sometimes even corrode their coworkers' attitudes. And to the extent that C players are taking up space, they block the advancement of stronger candidates.

So what do you do with them? In "A New Game Plan for C Players" (HBR January 2002), Beth Axelrod, Helen Handfield-Jones, and Ed Michaels suggest a tough but respectful approach: Give low performers a chance at redemption but set firm expectations to overcome procrastination and rationalization. Here's how:

- **Create a clear plan for improvement.** Employees won't improve in a vacuum. They need guidance on what to change and help changing it. Set concrete goals for them and have a well-defined end point. If C players don't meet agreed-upon standards within a specified amount of time, help them make a graceful, dignified exit. Make sure you've documented their progress, or lack thereof, so you don't take them by surprise or leave yourself open to any HR or legal battles.

- **Give candid, real-time feedback.** As difficult as it may be to provide critical feedback, you are doing C players no favors by withholding it. They need to understand if and how they're improving and where they're falling short. (See chapter 6, "Giving Feedback That Sticks.")

- **Provide a support network.** Don't invest a ton of your time coaching C players, but don't leave them to languish, either. You may want to rely on existing training programs or farm out the coaching, perhaps pairing the C player with a competent peer.

That's how to coach someone like Sam. If he doesn't make progress, don't let him stick around, no matter how nice he is and how hard he tries. The amount of time you give him will depend on the nature of his job and his commitment and capacity to improve. In most instances you'll know within a few months whether further investment will help. You need to move sensitively but swiftly in dealing with Sam. You owe it to Cindy and Ed—and to your organization—to focus your coaching efforts where they'll pan out.

Jim Grinnell is an associate professor of management at Merrimack College in North Andover, Massachusetts. His consulting firm, Grinnell Consulting, works with firms on leadership coaching and organizational change and development.

Chapter 13
Coaching Your Rookie Managers

by Carol A. Walker

Most organizations promote employees into managerial positions based on their technical competence. Very often, however, those people fail to grasp how their roles have changed—that their jobs are no longer about personal achievement but instead about enabling others to achieve, that sometimes driving the bus means taking a backseat, and that building a team is often more important than cutting a deal. Even the best employees can have trouble adjusting to these new realities. That trouble may be exacerbated by normal insecurities that make rookie managers hesitant to ask for help, even when they find themselves in thoroughly unfamiliar territory. As these new managers internalize their stress, their focus

Adapted from *Harvard Business Review,* April 2002 (product #R0204H)

becomes internal as well. They become insecure and self-focused and cannot properly support their teams. Inevitably, trust breaks down, staff members are alienated, and productivity suffers.

Many companies unwittingly support this downward spiral by assuming that their rookie managers will somehow learn critical management skills by osmosis. Some rookies do, to be sure, but in my experience they're the exceptions. Most need more help. In the absence of comprehensive training and intensive coaching—which most companies don't offer—the rookie manager's boss plays a key role. Of course, it's not possible for most senior managers to spend hours and hours every week overseeing a new manager's work, but if you know what typical challenges a rookie manager faces, you'll be able to anticipate some problems before they arise and nip others in the bud.

Delegating

Effective delegation may be one of the most difficult tasks for rookie managers. Senior managers bestow on them big responsibilities and tight deadlines, and they put a lot of pressure on them to produce results. The natural response of rookies when faced with such challenges is to "just do it," thinking that's what got them promoted in the first place. But their reluctance to delegate assignments also has its roots in some very real fears. First is the fear of losing stature: If I assign high-profile projects to my staff members, they'll get the credit. What kind of visibility will I be left with? Will it be clear to my boss and my staff what value I'm adding? Second is the fear of abdicating control: If I allow Frank to do this, how can

I be sure that he will do it correctly? In the face of this fear, the rookie manager may delegate tasks but supervise Frank so closely that he will never feel accountable. Finally, the rookie may be hesitant to delegate work because he's afraid of overburdening his staff. He may be uncomfortable assigning work to former peers for fear that they'll resent him. But the real resentment usually comes when staff members feel that lack of opportunity is blocking their advancement.

Signs that these fears may be playing out include new managers who work excessively long hours, are hesitant to take on new responsibilities, have staff members who seem unengaged, or have a tendency to answer on behalf of employees instead of encouraging them to communicate with you directly.

The first step toward helping young managers delegate effectively is to get them to understand their new role. Acknowledge that their job fundamentally differs from an individual contributor's. Clarify what you and the organization value in leaders. Developing talented, promotable staff is critical in any company. Let new managers know that they will be rewarded for these less tangible efforts in addition to hitting numerical goals. Understanding this new role is half the battle for rookie managers, and one that many companies mistakenly assume is evident from the start.

After clarifying how your rookie manager's role has changed, you can move on to tactics.

When a new manager grumbles about mounting workloads, seize the opportunity to discuss delegation. Encourage him to take small risks initially, playing to the obvious strengths of his staff members. Early successes will build the manager's confidence and willingness to take progressively larger risks in stretching each team member's capabilities. Reinforce to him that delegation does not mean abdication. Breaking a complex project into manageable chunks, each with clearly defined milestones, makes effective follow-up easier. It's also important to schedule regular meetings before the project even begins in order to ensure that the manager stays abreast of progress and that staff members feel accountable.

One young manager I worked with desperately needed to find time to train and supervise new employees. His firm had been recently acquired, and he had to deal with high staff turnover and new industrywide rules and regulations. The most senior person on his staff—a woman who had worked for the acquiring company—was about to return from an extended family leave, and he was convinced that he couldn't ask her for help. After all, she had a part-time schedule, and she'd asked to be assigned to the company's largest client. To complicate matters, he suspected that she resented his promotion. As we evaluated the situation, the manager was able to see that the senior staffer's number one priority was reestablishing herself as an important part of the team. Once he realized this, he asked her to take on critical supervisory responsibilities, balanced with a smaller client load, and she eagerly agreed. Indeed, she returned from leave excited about partnering with her manager to develop the team.

Getting Support from Above

Most first-time managers see their relationship with their boss more as one of servitude than of partnership. They will wait for you to initiate meetings, ask for reports, and question results. You may welcome this restraint, but generally it's a bad sign. For one thing, it puts undue pressure on you to keep the flow of communication going. Even more important, it prevents new managers from looking to you as a critical source of support. If they don't see you that way, it's unlikely that they will see themselves that way for their own people. The problem isn't only that your position intimidates them; it's also that they fear being vulnerable. A newly promoted manager doesn't want you to see weaknesses, lest you think you made a mistake in promoting her. When I ask rookie managers about their relationships with their bosses, they often admit that they are trying to "stay under the boss's radar" and are "careful about what [they] say to the boss."

Some inexperienced managers will not seek your help even when they start to founder. Seemingly capable rookie managers often try to cover up a failing project or relationship—just until they can get it back under control.

What's the boss of a rookie manager to do? You can begin by clarifying expectations. Explain the connection between the rookie's success and your success so that she understands that open communication is necessary for you to achieve your goals. Explain that you don't expect her to have all the answers. Introduce her to other managers within the company who may be helpful, and encourage her to contact them as needed. Let her know that mistakes happen but that the cover-up is always worse than the crime. Let her know that you like to receive occasional lunch invitations as much as you like to extend them.

Lunch and drop-by meetings are important, but they usually aren't enough. Consider meeting regularly with a new manager—perhaps weekly in the early stages of a new assignment, moving to biweekly or monthly as her confidence builds. These meetings will develop rapport, provide you with insight into how the person is approaching the job, and make the new manager organize her thoughts on a regular basis. Be clear that the meetings are her time and that it's up to her to plan the agenda. The message you send is that the individual's work is important to you and that you're a committed business partner. More subtly, you're modeling how to simultaneously empower and guide direct reports.

Projecting Confidence

Looking confident when you don't feel confident—it's a challenge we all face, and as senior managers we're usually conscious of the need when it arises. Rookie managers are often so internally focused that they are unaware of this need or the image they project. They are so focused on substance that they forget that form counts, too. The first weeks and months on the job are a critical time for new leaders to reach out to staff. If they don't project confidence, they are unlikely to inspire and energize their teams.

I routinely work with new managers who are unaware that their everyday demeanor is hurting their organizations. In one rapidly growing technology company, the service manager, Linda, faced high levels of stress. Service outages were all too common, and they were beyond her control. Customers were exacting, and they too were under great pressure. Her rapidly growing staff was generally inexperienced. Distraught customers and employees had her tied up in knots almost daily. She consistently appeared breathless, rushed, and fearful that the other shoe was about to drop. The challenge was perhaps too big for a first-time manager, but that's what happens in rapidly growing companies. On one level, Linda was doing an excellent job keeping the operation going. The client base was growing and retention was certainly high—largely as a result of her energy and resourcefulness. But on another level, she was doing a lot of damage.

Linda's frantic demeanor had two critical repercussions. First, she had unwittingly defined the standard for acceptable conduct in her department, and her inexperienced staff began to display the same behaviors. Before long, other departments were reluctant to communicate with Linda or her team, for fear of bothering them or eliciting an emotional reaction. But for the company to arrive at real solutions to the service problems, departments needed to openly exchange information, and that wasn't happening. Second, Linda was not portraying herself to senior managers as promotion material. They were pleased with her troubleshooting abilities, but they did not see a confident, thoughtful senior manager in the making. The image Linda was projecting would ultimately hold back both her career and her department.

Not all rookie managers display the problems that Linda did. Some appear excessively arrogant. Others wear their self-doubt on their sleeves. Whether your managers appear overwhelmed, arrogant, or insecure, honest feedback is your best tool. You can help rookie managers by telling them that it's always safe to let out their feelings— in your office, behind closed doors. Reinforce just how long a shadow they cast once they assume leadership positions. Their staff members watch them closely, and if they see professionalism and optimism, they are likely to demonstrate those characteristics as well. Preach the gospel of conscious comportment—a constant awareness of the image one is projecting to the world. If you observe a manager projecting a less-than-positive image, tell that person right away.

Just-in-time coaching is often the most effective method for showing rookie managers how to project confidence. For instance, the first time you ask a new manager to carry out an initiative, take a little extra time to walk her through the process. Impress upon her the cardinal rule of management: Your staff members don't necessarily have to like you, but they do need to trust you. Ensure that the new manager owns the message she's delivering.

Focusing on the Big Picture

Rookie managers have a real knack for allowing immediate tasks to overshadow overarching initiatives. This is particularly true for those promoted from within, because they've just come from the front lines where they're accustomed to constant firefighting. As a recent individual contributor armed with plenty of technical know-how, the rookie manager instinctively runs to the immediate rescue of any client or staff member in need. The sense of accomplishment rookies get from such rescues is seductive and far more exhilarating than rooting out the cause of all the firefighting. And what could be better for team spirit than having the boss jump into the trenches and fight the good fight?

Of course, a leader shows great team spirit if he joins the troops in emergencies. But are all those emergencies true emergencies? Are newer staff members being empowered to handle complex challenges? And if the rookie manager is busy fighting fires, who is thinking strategically for the department? If you're the senior manager and these questions are popping into your head, you may well have a rookie manager who doesn't fully understand his role or is afraid to seize it.

I recently worked with a young manager who had become so accustomed to responding to a steady flow of problems that he was reluctant to block off any time to work on the strategic initiatives we had identified. When I probed, he revealed that he felt a critical part of his role was to wait for crises to arise. "What if I schedule this time and something urgent comes up and I disappoint someone?" he asked. When I pointed out that he could always postpone his strategy sessions if a true emergency arose, he seemed relieved. But he saw the concept of making time to think about the business as self-indulgent—this, despite the fact that his group was going to be asked to raise productivity significantly in the following fiscal year, and he'd done nothing to prepare for that reality.

As a senior manager, you can help your rookies by explaining to them that strategic thinking is a necessary skill for career advancement: For first-time managers, 10% of the work might be strategic and 90% tactical. As executives climb the corporate ladder, however, those percentages will flip-flop. To be successful at the next level, managers must demonstrate that they can think and act strategically. You can use your regularly scheduled meetings to help your managers focus on the big picture. Don't allow them to simply review the latest results and move on. Ask probing questions about those results. For example, "What trends are you seeing in the marketplace that could affect you in two quarters? Tell me how your competition is responding to those same trends." Don't let them regale you with the wonderful training their staffs have been getting without asking, "What additional skills do we need to build in the staff to increase productivity by 25% next year?" If you aren't satisfied with your managers' responses, let them know that you expect them to think this way—not to have all the answers, but to be fully engaged in the strategic thought process.

Giving Constructive Feedback

It's human nature to avoid confrontations, and most people feel awkward when they have to correct others' behavior or actions. Rookie managers are no exception, and they often avoid addressing important issues with their staff.

You can help by creating an environment in which constructive feedback is perceived not as criticism but as a source of empowerment. This begins with the feedback you offer to your managers about their own development.

Often, brainstorming sessions can help rookie managers see that sticky personal issues can be broken down into straightforward business issues. Recommending a change in action is much easier than recommending a change in attitude. Never forget the old saw: You can't ask people to change their personalities, but you can ask them to change their behaviors.

Indeed, you should share your own techniques for dealing with difficult conversations. One manager I worked with became defensive whenever a staff member questioned her judgment. She didn't really need me to tell her that her behavior was undermining her image and effectiveness. She did need me to offer her some techniques that would enable her to respond differently in the heat of the moment. She trained herself to respond quickly and earnestly with a small repertoire of questions like, "Can you tell me more about what you mean by that?" This simple technique bought her the time she needed to gather her thoughts and engage in an interchange that was productive rather than defensive. She was too close to the situation to come up with the technique herself.

Delegating, thinking strategically, communicating—you may think this all sounds like Management 101. And you're right. The most basic elements of management are often what trip up managers early in their careers. And because they are the basics, the bosses of rookie managers often take them for granted. They shouldn't—an extraordinary number of people fail to develop these skills. I've maintained an illusion throughout this article—that only rookie managers suffer because they haven't mastered these core skills. But the truth is, managers at all levels make these mistakes. An organization that supports its new managers by helping them to develop these skills will have surprising advantages over the competition.

———————

Carol A. Walker is the president of Prepared to Lead (www.preparedtolead.com), a management consulting firm devoted to helping organizations maximize the effectiveness of first-time managers. Before founding the company, she worked for 15 years as an executive in the insurance and technology industries.

Chapter 14
Coaching Rising Managers to Emotional Maturity

by Kerry A. Bunker, Kathy E. Kram, and Sharon Ting

In the past 10 years, we've met dozens of managers who have fallen victim to a harmful mix of their own ambition and their bosses' willingness to overlook a lack of people skills. Indeed, most executives seek out smart, aggressive people, paying more attention to their accomplishments than to their emotional maturity. What's more, they know that their strongest performers have options—if they don't get the job they want at one company, they're bound to get it somewhere else. Why risk losing them to a competitor by delaying a promotion?

Adapted from *Harvard Business Review*, December 2002 (product #R0212F)

The answer is that promoting them can be just as risky. Putting these unseasoned managers into positions of authority too quickly robs them of the opportunity to develop the emotional competencies that come with time and experience—competencies like the ability to negotiate with peers, regulate their emotions in times of crisis, or win support for change. You may be delighted with such managers' intelligence and passion—and may even see younger versions of themselves—but peers and subordinates are more likely to see them as arrogant and inconsiderate, or, at the very least, aloof. And therein lies the problem. At some point in a young manager's career, usually at the vice president level, raw talent and determined ambition become less important than the ability to influence and persuade. And unless senior executives appreciate this fact and make emotional competence a top priority, these high-potential managers will continue to fail, often at significant cost to the company.

Research has shown that the higher a manager rises in the ranks, the more important soft leadership skills are to his success.[1] Our colleagues at the Center for Creative Leadership have found that about a third of senior executives derail or plateau at some point, most often due to an emotional deficit such as the inability to build a team or regulate their own emotions in times of stress. And in our combined 55 years of coaching and teaching, we've seen firsthand how a young manager risks his career when he fails to develop emotional competencies. But the problem isn't youth per se. The problem is a lack of emotional maturity, which doesn't come easily or automatically and isn't something you learn from a book. It's one thing to understand the importance of relationships at an intellectual level and to learn techniques like active listening; it's another matter entirely to develop a full range of interpersonal competencies like patience, openness, and empathy. Emotional maturity involves a fundamental shift in self-awareness and behavior, and that change requires practice, diligence, and time.

This article will look at five strategies for boosting emotional competencies and redirecting managers who are paying a price for damaged or nonexistent relationships. The strategies aren't terribly complicated, but implementing them and getting people to change their entrenched behaviors can be very difficult. Many of these managers are accustomed to receiving accolades, and it often isn't easy for them to hear—or act on—difficult messages. You may have to satisfy yourself with small victories and accept occasional slipups. But perhaps the greatest challenge is having the discipline to resist the charm of the young and the clueless—to refrain from promoting them before they are ready and to stay the course even if they threaten to quit.

Deepen 360-Degree Feedback

With its questionnaires and standardized rating scales, 360-degree feedback as it is traditionally implemented may not be sufficiently specific or detailed to get the attention of inexperienced managers who excel at bottom-line measures but struggle with more subtle relationship challenges. These managers will benefit from a deeper and more thorough process that includes time for reflection and follow-up conversations. That means, for example, interviewing a wider range of the manager's peers and subordinates and giving her the opportunity to read verbatim responses to open-ended questions. Such detailed and extensive feedback can help a person see herself more as others do, a must for the young manager lacking the self-awareness to understand where she's falling short.

We witnessed this lack of self-awareness in Bill Miller, a 42-year-old vice president at a software company—an environment where technical ability is highly prized (as with all the examples in these pages, we've changed Miller's name and other identifying features to protect our clients' identities). Miller had gone far on pure intellect, but he never fully appreciated his own strengths. So year after year, in assignment after assignment, he worked doubly hard at learning the complexities of the business, neglecting his relationships with his colleagues as an unintended consequence. His coworkers considered his smarts and business acumen among the finest in the company, but they found him unapproachable and detached. As a result, top management questioned his ability to lead the type of strategic change that would require motivating staff at all levels. Not until Miller went through an in-depth 360-degree developmental review was he able to accept that he no longer needed to prove his intelligence—that he could relax in that respect and instead work on strengthening his personal connections. After months of working hard to cultivate stronger relationships with his employees, Miller began to notice that he felt more included in chance social encounters like hallway conversations.

Art Grainger, a 35-year-old senior manager at a cement and concrete company, was generally considered a champion by his direct reports. He was also known for becoming defensive whenever his peers or superiors questioned or even discussed his unit's performance. Through 360-degree reviews, he discovered that while everyone saw him as committed, results-oriented, and technically brilliant, they also saw him as overly protective, claiming he resisted any action or decision that might affect his department. Only when Grainger heard that his staff agreed with what his bosses had been telling him for years did he concede that he needed to change. Since then, he has come to see members of other departments as potential allies and has tried to redefine his team to include people from across the company.

It's worth noting that many of these smart young managers aren't used to hearing criticism. Consequently, they may discount negative feedback, either because the comments don't mesh with what they've heard in previous conversations or because their egos are so strong. Or they may conclude that they can "fix" the problem right away—after all, they've been able to fix most problems they've encountered in the past. But developing emotional competencies requires practice and ongoing personal interactions. The good news is that if you succeed in convincing them that these issues are career threatening, they may apply the same zeal to their emotional development that they bring to their other projects. And that's why 360-degree feedback is so valuable: When it comes from multiple sources and is ongoing, it's difficult to ignore.

Interrupt the Ascent

When people are continually promoted within their areas of expertise, they don't have to stray far from their comfort zones, so they seldom need to ask for help, especially if they're good problem solvers. Accordingly, they may become overly independent and fail to cultivate relationships with people who could be useful to them in the future. What's more, they may rely on the authority that comes with rank rather than learning how to influence people.

We sometimes counsel our clients to broaden young managers' skills by assigning them to cross-functional roles outside their expected career paths. This is distinct from traditional job rotation, which has employees spending time in different functional areas to enhance and broaden their knowledge of the business. Rather, the manager is assigned a role in which he doesn't have much direct authority. This will help him focus on developing other skills like negotiation and influencing peers.

Such cross-functional assignments—with no clear authority or obvious ties to a career path—can be a tough sell. It's not easy to convince young managers that these assignments are valuable, nor is it easy to help them extract relevant knowledge.

Act on Your Commitment

One of the reasons employees get stuck in the pattern we've described is that their bosses point out deficits in emotional competencies but don't follow through. They either neglect to articulate the consequences of continuing the destructive behavior or make empty threats but proceed with a promotion anyway. The hard-charging young executive can only conclude that these competencies are optional.

A cautionary tale comes from Mitchell Geller who, at 29, was on the verge of being named partner at a law firm. He had alienated many of his peers and subordinates over the years through his arrogance, a shortcoming duly noted on his yearly performance reviews, yet his keen legal mind had won him promotion after promotion. With Geller's review approaching, his boss, Larry Snow, pointed to heavy attrition among the up-and-coming lawyers who worked for Geller and warned him that further advancement would be contingent on a change in personal style. Geller didn't take the feedback to heart— he was confident that he'd get by, as he always had, on sheer talent. And true to form, Snow didn't stick to his guns. The promotion came through even though Geller's behavior hadn't changed. Two weeks later, Geller, by then a partner responsible for managing client relationships, led meetings with two key accounts. Afterward, the first client approached Snow and asked him to sit in on future meetings. Then the second client withdrew his business altogether, complaining that Geller had refused to listen to alternative points of view.

Contrast Geller's experience with that of 39-year-old Barry Kessler, a senior vice president at an insurance company. For years, Kessler had been heir apparent to the CEO due to his strong financial skills and vast knowledge of the business—that is, until John Mason, his boss and the current CEO, began to question the wisdom of promoting him.

While Kessler managed his own group exceptionally well, he avoided collaboration with other units, which was particularly important as the company began looking for new growth opportunities, including potential alliances with other organizations. The problem wasn't that Kessler was hostile, it was that he was passively disengaged—a flaw that hadn't seemed as important when he was responsible only for his own group. In coaching Kessler, we learned that he was extremely averse to conflict and that he avoided situations where he couldn't be the decision maker. His aversions sharply limited his ability to work with peers.

Mason sent a strong signal, not only to Kessler but to others in the organization, when he essentially demoted Kessler by taking away some of his responsibilities and temporarily pulling him from the succession plan. To give Kessler an opportunity to develop the skills he lacked, Mason asked him to lead a cross-functional team dedicated to finding strategic opportunities for growth. Success would require Kessler to devote more time to developing his interpersonal skills. He had no authority over the other team members, so he had to work through disputes and help the team arrive at a consensus. Two years later, Kessler reports that he is more comfortable with conflict and feedback, and he's worked his way back into the succession plan.

Institutionalize Personal Development

One of the most effective ways to build managers' emotional competencies is to weave interpersonal goals into the fabric of the organization, where everyone is expected to demonstrate a specific set of emotional skills and where criteria for promotion include behaviors as well as technical ability. A built-in process will make it easier to uncover potential problems early and reduce the chances that people identified as needing personal development will feel singled out or unfairly held back. Employees will know exactly what's expected of them and what it takes to advance in their careers.

At one company where the senior management team committed to developing the emotional competencies of the company's leaders, the team first provided extensive education on coaching to the HR department, which in turn supervised a program whereby top managers coached their younger and more inexperienced colleagues. The goal was to have both the experienced and inexperienced benefit: The junior managers provided feedback on the senior people's coaching skills, and the senior people helped foster emotional competencies in their less experienced colleagues.

The results were encouraging. Wes Burke, an otherwise high-performing manager, had recently been struggling to meet his business targets. After spending time with Burke and conferring with his subordinates and peers, his coach (internal to the organization) came to believe that, in his zest to achieve his goals, Burke was unable to slow down and listen to other people's ideas. Burke wasn't a boor: He had taken courses in communication and knew how to fake listening behaviors such as nodding his head and giving verbal acknowledgments, but he was often distracted and not really paying attention. He never accepted this feedback until one day, while he was walking purposefully through the large operations plant he managed, a floor supervisor stopped him to discuss his ideas for solving an ongoing production problem. Burke flipped on his active-listening mode. After uttering a few acknowledgments and saying, "Thanks, let's talk more about that," he moved on, leaving the supervisor feeling frustrated and at a loss for how to capture his boss's interest. As it happened, Burke's coach was watching. He pulled the young manager aside and said, "You didn't hear a word Karl just said. You weren't really listening." Burke admitted as much to himself and his coach. He then apologized to Karl, much to the supervisor's surprise. Keeping this incident in mind helped Burke remember the importance of his working relationships. His coach had also helped him realize that he shouldn't have assumed his sheer will and drive would somehow motivate his employees. Burke had been wearing people down, physically and psychologically. A year later, Burke's operation was hitting its targets, an accomplishment he partially attributes to the one-on-one coaching he received.

Cultivate Informal Networks

While institutionalized programs to build emotional competencies are critical, some managers will benefit more from an informal network of relationships that fall outside the company hierarchy. Mentoring, for example, can help both junior and senior managers further their emotional development through a new type of relationship. And when the mentoring experience is a positive one, it often acts as a springboard to a rich variety of relationships with others throughout the organization. In particular, it gives junior managers a chance to experience different leadership styles and exposes them to diverse viewpoints.

Sonia Greene, a 32-year-old manager at a consulting firm, was hoping to be promoted to principal, but she hadn't raised the issue with her boss because she assumed he didn't think she was ready, and she didn't want to create tension. She was a talented consultant with strong client relationships, but her internal relationships were weak due to a combination of shyness, an independent nature, and a distaste for conflict, which inhibited her from asking for feedback. When her company launched a mentoring program, Greene signed up, and through a series of lengthy conversations with Jessica Burnham, a partner at the firm, she developed new insights about her strengths and weaknesses. The support of an established player such as Burnham helped Greene become more confident and honest in her development discussions with her boss, who hadn't been aware that Greene was willing to receive and act on feedback. Today, Greene is armed with a precise understanding of what she needs to work on and is well on her way to being promoted. What's more, her relationship with Burnham has prompted her to seek out other connections, including a peer group of up-and-coming managers who meet monthly to share experiences and offer advice to one another.

Delaying a promotion can be difficult given the steadfast ambitions of the young executive and the hectic pace of organizational life, which makes personal learning seem like an extravagance. It requires a delicate balance of honesty and support, of patience and goading. It means going against the norm of promoting people almost exclusively on smarts, talent, and business results. It also means contending with the disappointment of an esteemed subordinate.

But taking the time to build people's emotional competencies isn't an extravagance; it's critical to developing effective leaders. Give in to the temptation to promote your finest before they're ready, and you're left with executives who may thrive on change and demonstrate excellent coping and survival skills but who lack the self-awareness, empathy, and social abilities required to foster and nurture those strengths in others. MBA programs and management books can't teach young executives everything they need to know about people skills. Indeed, there's no substitute for experience, reflection, feedback, and, above all, practice.

Kerry A. Bunker is president of the leadership learning firm Mangrove Leadership Solutions, LLC and a senior fellow at both the Center for Creative Leadership and The Conference Board. **Kathy E. Kram** is the R.C. Shipley Professor in Management and Professor of Organizational Behavior, Boston University. At the time of original publication, **Sharon Ting** was a manager of the Awareness Program for Executive Excellence at the Center for Creative Leadership in Greensboro, North Carolina.

NOTE

1. In his HBR articles "What Makes a Leader" (November–December 1998) and "Primal Leadership: The Hidden Driver of Great Performance" (with Richard Boyatzis and Annie McKee, December 2001), Daniel Goleman makes the case that emotional competence is the crucial driver of a leader's success.

Chapter 15
Coaching Teams

by J. Richard Hackman

Team coaching is about group processes. It involves direct interaction with a team that is intended to help members use their collective resources well in accomplishing work. Examples of coaching include leading a launch meeting before work begins (which can help members become oriented to and engaged with their task), providing the team feedback about its problem analysis (which can increase the quality of its analytic work), or asking a team reflective questions about why members made a particular decision (which can help them make better use of their knowledge and experience). By contrast, a leader who personally coordinates the work of a team or who negotiates outside resources for its use is doing things that can be quite helpful to the team—but he or she is

Adapted from *Leading Teams: Setting the Stage for Great Performances* (product #3332), by J. Richard Hackman, Harvard Business Review Press, 2002, pp. 165–196.

not coaching. Coaching is about building teamwork, not about doing the team's work.

Coaching can address any aspect of team interaction that is impeding members' ability to work well together or that shows promise of strengthening team functioning. In practice, however, a more focused approach brings better results. Research has identified three aspects of group interaction that have special leverage in shaping team effectiveness: the amount of effort members apply to their collective work, the appropriateness to the task and situation of the performance strategies they employ in carrying out the work, and the level of knowledge and skill they apply to the work.[1]

Process Losses and Gains

All task-performing teams encounter what psychologist Ivan Steiner calls "process losses," and can all potentially create synergistic process gains. Process losses are inefficiencies or internal breakdowns that keep a group from doing as well as it theoretically could, given its resources and member talents.[2] They develop when members interact in ways that depress the team's effort, the appropriateness of its strategy, or the utilization of member talent, and they waste or misapply member time, energy, and expertise. Process gains develop when members interact in ways that enhance collective effort, generate uniquely appropriate strategies for working together, or actively develop members' knowledge and skills. When this happens, the team has created new internal resources that can be used in its work, capabilities that did not exist be-

TABLE 15-1

Characteristic process losses and gains for each of the three performance processes

Effort

Process loss: "Social loafing" by team members
Process gain: Development of high shared commitment to the team and its work

Performance strategy

Process loss: Mindless reliance on habitual routines
Process gain: Invention of innovative, task-appropriate work procedures

Knowledge and skill

Process loss: Inappropriate weighting of member contributions
Process gain: Sharing of knowledge and development of member skills

---

fore the team created them. As seen in table 15-1, there are special kinds of process losses and process gains associated with each of the three performance processes we have identified.

What Coaches Do and When They Do It

A coaching intervention is any action that seeks to minimize process losses or to foster process gains for any of the three key performance processes. Coaching that addresses effort is motivational in character; its functions are to minimize free riding and to build shared commitment to the group and its work. Coaching that addresses performance strategy is consultative in character; its functions are to minimize thoughtless reliance on habitual routines and to foster the invention of ways of proceeding with the work that are especially well aligned with task and situational requirements and opportunities. Coaching that addresses knowledge and skill is educational in character; its functions are to minimize suboptimal weighting of members' contributions and to foster the development of members' knowledge and skill.

Coaching that succeeds in reducing losses or fostering gains for one or more of the three performance processes virtually always contributes to overall team effectiveness. This kind of coaching can be done by anyone (including rank-and-file team members, external managers, and outside consultants—not just a person officially designated as "team leader"), and it can be provided at any time in the course of a team's work. There are, nonetheless, three particular times in a team's life when members are likely to be especially receptive to each of the three types of coaching interventions. And, as we will see, there are other times in a team's life cycle when even competent coaching is unlikely to make much of a difference in how well members work together.

The findings of organizational psychologist Connie Gersick are especially useful in explaining why certain kinds of coaching interventions are uniquely helpful at different times in the team life cycle. In a field study of the life histories of a number of task-performing teams, Gersick found that each of the groups she tracked developed a distinctive approach toward its task as soon as it commenced work, and stayed with that approach until almost exactly halfway between its first meeting and its project deadline.[3] At the midpoint of their lives, all teams underwent a major transition. In a concentrated burst of changes, they dropped old patterns of behavior, reengaged with outside supervisors, and adopted new perspectives on their work. Following the midpoint transition, groups entered a period of focused task execution, which persisted until very near the project deadline, at which time a new set of issues having to do with termination processes arose and captured members' attention.

Gersick's findings suggest that when a team is just starting a new piece of work, members may be especially open to interventions that address their level of engagement with the team and its work. The midpoint, when half the allotted time has elapsed (or, perhaps, the work is half done), is a uniquely appropriate time for interventions that help members reflect on how well their performance strategies are working, and to change them if needed. And the end, when a work cycle has been completed, is the time when a team is ready to entertain interventions aimed at helping members learn from their experiences. The proper times for motivational, consultative, and educational interventions are summarized in figure 15-1.[4]

FIGURE 15-1

The temporal appropriateness of coaching interventions

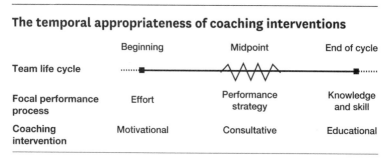

	Beginning	Midpoint	End of cycle
Team life cycle			
Focal performance process	Effort	Performance strategy	Knowledge and skill
Coaching intervention	Motivational	Consultative	Educational

Beginnings

There is much on a team's plate when members first come together to perform a piece of work—establishing the boundary that distinguishes members from nonmembers, starting to formulate member roles and behavioral norms, and engaging with (and, inevitably, redefining) the group task. Members' decisions about such matters, whether made explicitly or implicitly, establish a track for the group on which members stay for a considerable time.[5] A coaching intervention that helps a team have a good launch increases the chances that the track will be one that enhances members' commitment to the team and motivation for its work.

The leader's behavior at the launch meeting of any type of work team serves to breathe life into the team's structural shell, no matter how rudimentary it may be, and thereby help the team start functioning on its own. If the launch meeting is successful, the team leader will have helped the team move from being just a list of names to being a real, bounded social system. The official task that the team was assigned will have been examined, assessed, and then redefined to become the slightly different task that members actually work on.[6] And the norms of conduct specified by those who created the team will have been assessed, tried out (sometimes explicitly but more often implicitly through members' behaviors), and gradually revised and made the team's own.

Midpoints

The midpoint of a team's life cycle, when a team is likely to experience a naturally occurring upheaval in how members are relating to one another and to their work, turns out to be an especially good time for a coaching intervention that invites them to reflect on the team's performance strategy. At such times (or at other natural breakpoints or low-workload periods), coaching interventions that encourage members to mindfully reflect on their work thus far and on the challenges they next will face can be quite helpful to them in revising and improving their plans for the next phase of their work.

Research by organizational psychologist Anita Woolley provides compelling support for this proposition. She devised an experimental version of an architectural task, involving construction of a college residence hall out of LEGO bricks. Groups were informed in advance how the structures they created would be evaluated, on dimensions that included sturdiness (assessed using a "drop test" unique in the annals of architecture), aesthetics, and technical indices involving floor space, number of floors, and so on. She devised two coaching-type interventions, one intended to improve members' interpersonal relations, and another that provided assistance to the team in developing a task-appropriate performance strategy. Each team received only one intervention, which was administered either at the beginning or at the midpoint of its work period.[7]

Woolley's findings, shown in figure 15-2, confirm that strategy interventions are especially helpful when they come near the midpoint of a team's work cycle. When the strategy intervention was administered at the beginning of the work period, before members had logged some experience with the task, it did not help. Note also that the intervention that addressed members' interpersonal

FIGURE 15-2

Coaching type and timing

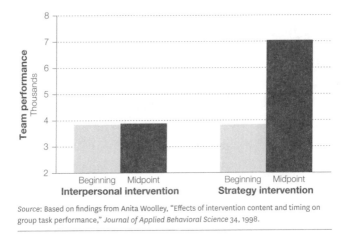

Source: Based on findings from Anita Woolley, "Effects of intervention content and timing on group task performance," *Journal of Applied Behavioral Science* 34, 1998.

relationships rather than their task processes made no difference whatever in team performance, regardless of when it was administered—an important finding to which we will return shortly.

Coaching about performance strategy helps team members stay closely in touch with changing demands and opportunities in their environment and encourages them to find ways to implement their chosen performance strategies mindfully and efficiently. Strategy-focused coaching can also help members find or invent new performance strategies that are more appropriate to the task and environment than those they had previously been using. It can even prompt a team to engage in some persuasion or political action to try to negotiate a change in organizational constraints that may be impeding their performance.

Endings

Because focus on the project dissipates somewhat once a piece of work is finished, postperformance periods offer an especially good time for coaching interventions aimed at helping members capture and internalize the lessons that can be learned from their work experiences. Even then, however, team members may be disinclined to exploit the learning opportunities that are available to them. When a team learns that it has performed splendidly—for example, an athletic team that has won the championship game or a task force whose project proposal has been approved—members may be much more disposed to celebrate their success than to explore what they can learn from their experience. Celebration is to be valued because it confirms that the team has done well and it fosters collective internal motivation. But if receiving positive performance feedback prompts nothing more than that, members may fail to notice those aspects of the feedback that could help them learn how to work together even more effectively in the future. It is fine for a basketball team to hoist the coach to members' shoulders to cut the net from the hoop; but in the locker room later, or at practice the next day, the team should also take a few moments to reflect on the lessons to be learned from its victory.

What Good Coaches Don't Do

Although I am agnostic about the particular behaviors or styles coaches should exhibit, that is decidedly not the case regarding the focus of coaches' activities. That focus should be on a team's task performance processes, not on members' social interactions or interpersonal relationships. The great majority of writing about team coaching posits (sometimes explicitly but more often implicitly) that coaching interventions should foster smooth or harmonious relationships among team members. This emphasis on harmony is misplaced and derives from a logical fallacy about the role of interpersonal processes in shaping team performance outcomes.

When we observe a team that is having performance problems, we often simultaneously see a group that is plagued with interpersonal difficulties—conflict among members, leadership struggles, communications breakdowns, and so on. It is natural to infer that these difficulties are causing the performance problems and, therefore, that the best way to improve team performance would be to fix them. As reasonable and as consistent with lay experience as this inference is, it is neither logical nor correct. In fact, the causal arrow often points in the opposite direction—how a group is performing shapes the character of members' interaction rather than vice versa. Or at least it shapes members' perceptions of their interaction. Social psychologist Barry Staw gave teams false feedback about their performance and then asked members to provide objective descriptions of how the team had functioned. Teams that had been led to believe that they had performed well reported that their interaction had been more harmonious and that they had communicated better (among other differences) than did groups whose members thought they had performed poorly.[8]

As tempting as it may be for coaches to jump in and try to make things better when they observe members enmeshed in interpersonal conflicts or leadership struggles, there is little reason to believe that such interventions will succeed in clearing out the interpersonal underbrush so task work can get back on track. More advisable, perhaps, would be to address the structural or contextual conditions that may have engendered the interpersonal difficulties, and to supplement those structural improvements with well-timed and task-focused coaching of the kind described in this chapter.

Yet even teams that are appropriately structured and supported inevitably encounter some rough interpersonal sledding. Despite the pain that members may feel while experiencing and trying to resolve such problems, they are not necessarily bad for a group or detrimental to its performance. On the contrary, research shows that certain patterns of interaction that are often experienced as problematic by team members and coded the same way by outside observers can actually promote team performance and member learning.[9] Task-based conflict is one such pattern, and the vocal presence of a member with "deviant" views is another. A skilled coach knows that it sometimes is best to leave things alone and let the tension remain high for a while, rather than to rush in and try to contain the problems or refocus their most negative manifestations.

Sharing Coaching

Throughout this chapter, I have discussed coaching as if it were done by one person, perhaps someone designated as "team leader" or "team advisor" or, for that matter, "coach." In practice, coaching is often done by a number of individuals, sometimes different ones at different times or for different purposes—including, especially in mature self-managing teams, team members themselves. What is critical is that competent coaching be available to a team, regardless of who provides it or what formal positions those providers hold.

The potential benefits of sharing coaching among team members are wonderfully evidenced by the Orpheus Chamber Orchestra, a twenty-six-person ensemble that both rehearses and performs without a conductor. Although that orchestra has no leader on the podium, it has much more leadership than do orchestras known for their famous conductors.[10] For each piece of music the orchestra chooses to perform, one violinist is selected by his or her peers to serve as concertmaster. That person manages the rehearsal process for that piece—beginning each rehearsal, fielding suggestions from members about interpretive matters, deciding when spirited disagreements among members must be set aside to get on with the rehearsal, and taking the lead in figuring out how to handle transitions in the music that in a traditional orchestra would be signaled by a conductor's baton.

There is abundant shared leadership and peer-to-peer coaching in this unusual orchestra, but it is far from a one-person, one-vote democracy.[11] Orpheus members are quite discriminating about who is invited to have special say in the preparation of each piece. Only some violinists are chosen to serve as concertmasters, for example, and it is clear to all which members have earned the right to be listened to especially carefully about which musical issues. Members are not treated as equals because in fact they are not equals: Each individual brings special talents and interests to the ensemble and has also some areas of relative disinterest and lesser strength. Orpheus members recognize that fact and exploit it relentlessly in the interest of collective excellence. The orchestra's willingness to acknowledge, to respect, and to exploit the individual differences among its members is one of its greatest strengths as a self-managing team. It is as fine an example of shared leadership and peer coaching as I have encountered.

One of the things that helps peer coaching work so well at the Orpheus Chamber Orchestra is that those who are coaching are also playing in the orchestra, and therefore they are always there. It is difficult, if not impossible, for any of the three kinds of coaching explored in this chapter—motivational, consultative, and educational coaching—to be accomplished by remote control. Good coaching helps team members practice and learn the skills and rewards of being superb self-managers, and that is highly unlikely to happen if the coach is rarely around.[12]

J. Richard Hackman was one of the world's leading experts on group and organizational behavior and was a professor of social and organizational psychology at Harvard University.

NOTES

1. For details, see J. R. Hackman and C. G. Morris, "Group Tasks, Group Interaction Process, and Group Performance Effectiveness: A Review and Proposed Integration," in *Advances in Experimental Social Psychology* 8: 45–99, ed. L. Berkowitz (New York: Academic Press, 1975); and J. R. Hackman and R. Wageman, *A Theory of Team Coaching,* manuscript submitted for publication (2001).

2. For additional details about the origins, dynamics, and consequences of process losses in groups, see I. D. Steiner, *Group Process and Productivity* (New York: Academic Press, 1972).

3. Since the groups' projects in the original study [C. J. G. Gersick, "Time and Transition in Work Teams: Toward a New Model of Group Development," *Academy of Management Journal* 31 (1988): 9–41] were of varying duration, these periods varied from several days to several weeks. A subsequent experimental study [C. J. G. Gersick, "Marking Time: Predictable Transitions in Task Groups," *Academy of Management Journal* 31 (1989): 9–41], in which all groups had the same amount of time to complete their task, found the same life-cycle dynamics as did the original field study.

4. For details, including discussion of conditions under which time-inappropriate motivational, educational, and consultative coaching interventions may nonetheless succeed, see J. R. Hackman and R. Wageman, *A Theory of Team Coaching,* manuscript submitted for publication (2001). Timing issues in coaching teams are also explored in a teaching case and video; see R. Wageman and J. R. Hackman, "The Overhead Reduction Task Force" [Case No. 9-400-026], [Videocassette No. 9-400- 501], [Teaching Note No. 5-400-027] (Boston: Harvard Business School Publishing, 1999).

5. It is a characteristic of all social systems, from small groups to large organizations, that decisions made early in a system's life have consequences over its entire life span. See P. David, "Understanding the Economics of QWERTY: The Necessity of History," in *Economic History and the Modern Historian,* ed. W. Parker (London: Blackwell, 1986), 30–59; W. R. Scott, "Unpacking Institutional Arguments," in *The New Institutionalism in Organizational Analysis,* ed. W. W. Powell and P. J. DiMaggio (Chicago: University of Chicago Press, 1991), 164–182.

6. Although I am aware of no systematic research on the process by which work teams revise and redefine their assigned tasks, the task redefinition process has been examined for individual performers (see J. R. Hackman, "Toward Understanding the Role of Tasks in Behavioral Research," *Acta Psychologica* 31 (1969): 97–128; and B. M. Staw and R. D. Boettger, "Task Revision: A Neglected Form of Work Performance," *Academy of Management Journal* 33 (1990): 534–559).

7. For details, see A. W. Woolley, "Effects of Intervention Content and Timing on Group Task Performance," *Journal of Applied Behavioral Science* 34 (1998): 30–49.

8. For details, see B. M. Staw, "Attribution of the 'Causes' of Performance: A General Alternative Interpretation of Cross-Sectional Research on Organizations," *Organizational Behavior and Human Performance* 13 (1975): 414–432.

9. Two findings are of special interest in the present context. Jehn (1995) found that task conflict could facilitate group performance for engaging tasks, but that it impaired group functioning for tasks that were highly routine. This finding further affirms the interdependence between team structure (here, the design of its task) and group interaction processes. Coaching interventions that help team members identify and address differences in their views about how the task ought to be performed can be helpful if the team task is motivationally well designed—but can backfire if the task is routine and repetitive [K. A. Jehn, "A Multimethod Examination of the Benefits and Detriments of Intragroup Conflict," *Administrative Science Quarterly* 40 (1995): 256–282]. Research by Jehn and Mannix (2001) highlights the role of timing in understanding and addressing conflict among members. Among other findings, these researchers observed that well-performing teams exhibited moderate levels of task conflict at the midpoint of the group interaction. And, as we have seen, the midpoint is exactly the time when teams are most open to coaching interventions intended to help members bring their task performance strategies into better alignment with task and situational demands. [K. A. Jehn and E. A. Mannix, "The Dynamic Nature of Conflict: A Longitudinal Study of Intragroup Conflict and Group Performance," *Academy of Management Journal* 44 (2001): 238–251].

10. For details, see E. V. Lehman and J. R. Hackman, "The Orpheus Chamber Orchestra: Case and Video," Boston: Kennedy School of Government, Harvard University (2001); H. Seifter and P. Economy, *Leadership Ensemble* (New York: Henry Holt, 2001); and J. Traub, "Passing the Baton: What C.E.O.s Could Learn from the Orpheus Chamber Orchestra," *The New Yorker* (Aug. 26/Sept. 2 1996): 100–105.

11. The idea of shared leadership is generally more attractive in theory than it is in practice. Not to have some single individual who is responsible for making sure things stay on track is to invite coordination problems ("Who *was* supposed to do that?") and unnecessary interpersonal conflict as those who are supposedly sharing leadership arrange themselves into a hierarchy. Ideas such as "Co-CEOs" and the "Office of the President" sound better than they actually work.

12. It also is possible, of course, for a coach to be *oppressively* present. If the coach takes over and handles personally all the problems he or she believes to be really serious, then members will be unlikely to ever develop their collective capabilities as a self-managing team.

Index

Notes

Notes

Notes

Notes

Smart advice and inspiration from a source you trust.

If you enjoyed this book and want more comprehensive guidance on essential professional skills, turn to the HBR Guides Boxed Set. Packed with the practical advice you need to succeed, this seven-volume collection provides smart answers to your most pressing work challenges, from writing more effective emails and delivering persuasive presentations to setting priorities and managing up and across.

Harvard Business Review Guides

Available in paperback or ebook format. Plus, find downloadable tools and templates to help you get started.

- Better Business Writing
- Building Your Business Case
- Buying a Small Business
- Coaching Employees
- Delivering Effective Feedback
- Finance Basics for Managers
- Getting the Mentoring You Need
- Getting the Right Work Done

- Leading Teams
- Making Every Meeting Matter
- Managing Stress at Work
- Managing Up and Across
- Negotiating
- Office Politics
- Persuasive Presentations
- Project Management

HBR.ORG/GUIDES

Buy for your team, clients, or event.
Visit hbr.org/bulksales for quantity discount rates.

The most important management ideas all in one place.

We hope you enjoyed this book from *Harvard Business Review*. For the best ideas HBR has to offer turn to HBR's 10 Must Reads Boxed Set. From books on leadership and strategy to managing yourself and others, this 6-book collection delivers articles on the most essential business topics to help you succeed.

HBR's 10 Must Reads Series

The definitive collection of ideas and best practices on our most sought-after topics from the best minds in business.

- Change Management
- Collaboration
- Communication
- Emotional Intelligence
- Innovation
- Leadership
- Making Smart Decisions

- Managing Across Cultures
- Managing People
- Managing Yourself
- Strategic Marketing
- Strategy
- Teams
- The Essentials

hbr.org/mustreads

Buy for your team, clients, or event.
Visit hbr.org/bulksales for quantity discount rates.

Harvard
Business
Review
Press